Salon Promotions:
Creative Blueprints for Success

Salon Promotions:
Creative Blueprints for Success

by
Judy Ventura

Milady Publishing
(a division of Delmar Publishers)
3 Columbia Circle, P.O. Box 12519
Albany, New York 12212-2519

NOTICE TO THE READER

Cover Design: Spiral Design Studio

Milady Staff
Publisher: Gordon Miller
Acquisitions Editor: Joseph Miranda
Project Editor: NancyJean Downey
Production Manager: Brian Yacur
Production and Art/Design Coordinator: Suzanne Nelson

COPYRIGHT © 1998
Milady Publishing
(a division of Delmar Publishers)
an International Thomson Publishing company

Printed in the United States of America
Printed and distributed simultaneously in Canada

For more information, contact:
SalonOvations
Milady Publishing
3 Columbia Circle, Box 12519
Albany, New York 12212-2519

2 3 4 5 6 7 8 9 10   XXX   03 02 01 00 99 98

Library of Congress Cataloging-in-Publication Data

Ventura, Judy.
    Salon promotions: creative blueprints for success / by Judy Ventura.
        p.   cm.
    ISBN: 1-56253-350-9
        1. Beauty shops—United States—Marketing.   2. Beauty shops—United States—Management.
3. New business enterprises—United States—Marketing.   3. New business enterprises—
United States—Management.   I. Title.
TT965.V46 1997   97-10908
646.7'2'0688–dc21   CIP

contents

	Dedication	viii
	Preface	ix
Chapter 1	**Promoting Yourself in a New Salon**	**1**
	Objectives	1
	Key Terms	1
	Building a Clientele	1
	Fitting into the Salon Image	2
	Your Clientele	2
	Exposure	2
	Business Cards and Flyers	3
	Teamwork	5
	Summary	6
	Key Terms Defined	7
Chapter 2	**Know Your Market**	**8**
	Objectives	8
	Key Terms	8
	Who Are Your Salon's Clients?	8
	Upscale/Professional Salons	9
	Middle Income Salons	10
	Value-Priced Salons	14
	Specialty Salons	16
	Summary	20
	Key Terms Defined	20
Chapter 3	**Preparing for Salon Promotions**	**21**
	Objectives	21
	Key Terms	21
	Appearance and Potential	21
	Salon Appearance	22

Customer Service 22
Salon Potential 23
Your Business Plan 24
Mission Statement 27
Staff Training and Motivation 27
Contests 28
Staff Pictures and Videos 28
Brochures 29
Summary 30
Key Terms Defined 30

Chapter 4

**Courting Current Clients and
Retaining Them** **31**
Objectives 31
Key Terms 31
Customer Appreciation 31
Client Referral Cards 33
Client Records 33
Tracking Service and Product Sales 33
Client Concerns 34
Introducing New Services 35
Summary 36
Key Terms Defined 37

Chapter 5

Media Advertising **38**
Objectives 38
Key Terms 38
Advertising Agencies 39
Types of Media 40
Print Ads 40
Press Releases 41
Outdoor Advertising 41
Radio Ads 42
Television Ads 42
On-line Advertising 43
Other Advertising Methods 43
Coupons and Mail Offers 43
Point of Sale 44
Photographs 44
Summary 45
Key Terms Defined 45

Chapter 6

**Planning a Yearly Calendar of
Advertising Campaigns** **46**
Objectives 46
Key Terms 46
Monthly Promotions 46
Seasonal Promotions 47

Retail Promos   48
New-in-Town Promos   49
Telephone Cards   50
Summary   51
Key Terms Defined   51

Chapter 7

**Calculating the Cost for
Each Promotion   52**
Objectives   52
Key Terms   52
Percentage of Yearly Budget   52
Co-op Advertising Dollars   54
Calculating the Discount Percentage   54
Teaming Up with Other Stores   56
Bartering   56
Summary   57
Key Terms Defined   57

Chapter 8

**Are You Sure You Want to
Offer a Sale?   58**
Objectives   58
Key Terms   58
Sale Only Clientele   59
Selected Stylists Only   59
One Day Sales   60
Summary   62
Key Terms Defined   62

Chapter 9

Flyers, Flyers, Flyers   63
Objectives   63
Key Terms   63
Developing Flyers   63
Low Cost and High Return   64
Velox and Ad Slicks   64
Computer Graphics   64
Distributing Flyers   64
    Timing   64
    Location   65
Summary   66
Key Terms Defined   66

Chapter 10

Promotions   67

Glossary   402

Index   403

dedication

IF YOU ARE LUCKY, you have one hero in life! Someone who is a role model and a person to look up to and depend on. I have been lucky enough to have several heroes and I would like to dedicate this book to them, as a small token of appreciation for all that they add to my life!

First of all, to my mother, Adeline, a special thanks for being my strength, inspiration and my HERO.

Secondly, to my daughter, Gina, a special thanks for your love and support. I treasure you! You are my best girlfriend and my HERO!

To my sister, Ann, thanks for being the person I admire and respect most in life. I am proud of you and I am glad to call you, my HERO. Your strength and love are a monument to motherhood and family. Thanks for making all our lives better.

To my dear & sweet friend, Parker Washburn, owner of Leon's Beauty School and Salons, in Greensboro, NC, thanks for being a great inspiration to future cosmetologists. Your school is the standard from which all schools should be judged. Your insight, dedication, love, discipline and determination have helped thousands of young people find a wonderful and successful career. I am proud to work with you and to call you my friend and my HERO!

To my many friends that have suffered from AIDS; Michael, Rick, Page, Vermeil, Wyatt, Jerry...you are the real HEROES of the world. You have each been a special part of my life and I am richer for having known all of you!

Judy Ventura

preface

THIS TEXT IS WRITTEN primarily for use in promoting new salons. It is, however, useful for all hairstylists who wish to promote their business.

The text has been written so that even the more novice stylists can learn the basics of salon promotions, choose a promotion that suits their needs, and follow the easy instructions to use the promotion and track the results.

The text is primarily written into two sections. The first section, Chapters 1 to 9, explains how, where, and why promotions work.

The second section, Chapter 10, consists of more than 100 examples of handouts that you can actually use to promote your new salon.

In the 25 years that I (both as a cosmetologist and instructor) have used promotions, I have had fun and created business for myself and countless stylists who worked with me or were my students. I am sure that the promotions in this book will help to make your new salon a success, too!

Before using any promotions, stylists should always be sure to get the permission of the salon owner and manager.

The author wishes to thank Marlena Pratt, Joe Miranda, Nancy Downey, and all the staff at Milady for their continued support.

The publisher wishes to thank the following professioinals for reviewing this manuscript: Victoria Harper, Kokomo, IN.; Colleen Hennessey, Stamford, CT.; Lee Hoffman, Cuyahoga Falls, OH; and Maren Longergan, Bettendorf, IA.

promoting yourself in a new salon

IN THIS CHAPTER, YOU WILL LEARN:

- How to match your *personal image* with a *salon image*
- How to get *exposure*
- How to use *business cards* to promote yourself
- How *teamwork* helps to build your clientele

KEY TERMS

- exposure
- professional courtesy
- referrals
- salon image
- transient trade

CONGRATULATIONS! You have completed the required training and you have passed your state examination to become a cosmetologist. You have all the tools you need and you are ready to start work. However, you may find one more hurdle lies ahead of you! Starting your business can be a challenge. In a new salon, you may find that you do not have enough **transient trade** (walk-in clients) for your appointment book to stay as busy as you would like it to be and for you to earn the type of income you had envisioned.

Traditionally, it could take a couple of years for a stylist to generate enough request clientele to earn a good living. However, by using some simple promotional techniques, you could be successful in a relatively short time!

BUILDING A CLIENTELE

In building a successful clientele, you may want to direct your attention to four main areas: fitting into the salon image, clien-

1

tele, exposure, and printed promotional material.

Fitting Into the Salon Image

Every salon has its own **salon image** or personality! Some salons are extremely formal and quiet, some are chic and trendy, and still others are traditional or casual. Whichever type of salon you are working in, you will want to fit into the salon image. Be sure your dress, hair, nails, and makeup are indicative of the image the salon is trying to portray!

- It may be time for a makeover if you are wearing tennis shoes, jeans, and waist-length hair, yet your salon is trendy and promotes the latest styles and the newest colors before any other salon in town does!

- Perhaps you may be a trendsetter in your dress and hairstyle, but the salon offers a more traditional image to its clientele, which is primarily business professionals.

- If you are unsure which image your salon portrays, or how you should promote that image, ask the manager and salon owner to spend a few moments and give you an overview of the direction they see the salon moving in. Ask the manager how you fit into the salon's image and what can you do to blend your image with the salon's.

Your Clientele

In most cases, you will find that your clientele will be a reflection of you.

Therefore, the way you wear your hair, makeup, and nails will attract clients who want to wear the same style you do! If you are embarking on the road to success with last year's styles, it may be time you had a makeover! Again, consult the salon manager. Some salons offer makeover services for new stylists and in addition to it helping your image, it can be a way for the staff to bond and have a lot of fun, too! (Any type of service for another stylist may be performed at no charge and called a **professional courtesy**, but be sure to check out the financial terms before the makeover begins!)

Exposure

The second area that you may wish to direct your attention to is exposure. The word **exposure** means to reveal, publish, communicate, or unveil. That is exactly what you, as a new stylist, must do to build a clientele!

- You must *reveal* to the public that you are a new stylist who is talented and trained and ready to serve them.

- You must *publish* special offers and your array of services.

- You must *communicate* your availability and location and you must unveil yourself, your talents, and your skills to the world!

How do you do all this? By *promotions*, of course! In the following chapters, you will be able to decide on a promotion, prepare for it, enact the promotion, and track the results.

Exposure is important because it is the means by which the world finds out that the best stylist is working in your town, your salon, and your chair. When you present your talents and abilities through promotions, you will be selling yourself to the public. You are probably already familiar with some promotions. Large companies and manufacturers use coupons and give-aways to let you sample their soap that cleans the best, use their toothpaste that fights the most cavities, and test drive their new and unique car. Some promotional campaigns have been so successful that we have come to think of one particular brand name when a product is mentioned.

- The brand name Kleenex™ has been so successfully marketed, that we often call a facial tissue a Kleenex.
- The most popular instant camera is made by Polaroid™ company, and we call pictures any brand instant camera takes Polaroids.
- The frozen, colored, sugar water on a stick that makes zillions of kids happy every day is called? That's right, we call all the brands of frozen, fruit-flavored ice on a stick Popsicles™, don't we?

By promoting yourself and creating exposure for *your talents, your name could become synonymous with cosmetology!*

Business Cards and Flyers

Another area that requires a special effort is printed promotional material, more specifically, business cards and flyers. In Chapter 9 we discuss flyers at length, but for now, you need only be aware flyers are the least expensive way to promote yourself and expose your talents as well as your name to potential clients, while giving them the specific reasons that you are the *cosmetologist they have been searching for!*

Just like the advertisements that help you decide on a certain brand of laundry soap or the coupons we cut out of the newspaper to buy a brand of deodorant, your potential customers will look at your business cards and get an impression about you! Your business card is important and needs your consideration and planning. Many printing companies can design and print a card, or you may even design one yourself and just have some printed. Another choice is to have an artist design one for you. (You could have an art student design one for you in exchange for a haircut.) There are even software packages that you can load on your home computer, which allow you to create a masterpiece at home. Whichever you choose, remember that you want this card to stand out from all others. You also want to give your clients a reason to hold on to them. We all receive stacks of business cards and keep only the ones that interest us. As a new stylist, you must grab clients' interest and make them want to keep your card! Let's look at some business cards (Figures 1-1, 1-2, and 1-3) and the messages they portray to potential clients.

1. Look at the first business card. It has the stylist's name and salon address and number, but it lacks pizzazz. It may not be saved by the client you hand it to.

FIGURE 1-1 Business card

FIGURE 1-2 Business card offering money off a service

Borrow Ideas From Successful Stylists!

- A successful stylist once made magnets from her business card—perfect for the refrigerator.
- Another stylist prints a yearly calendar on the back of her card.
- A top stylist once printed a place to write client appointments on the back of cards.
- Definitely use color business cards; top salons usually do! They attract more attention and, after all, we are in the business of beauty and color.
- Some stylists have a fold-open card that has room to write retail prescriptions and suggestions for future services. This type of card would be great to give out after consultations.
- Some successful stylists make their business cards a punch card. For each service the customer receives, the card is punched. Customers receive a free gift or service when they have completed the card punches.

2. Card number two offers a $10 discount *if you present the card*, so many more clients will hold on to the card.

3. Card number three gives the client a reason to call you: you are offering to fulfill their

TRY ON THE COLOR YOU'VE ALWAYS DREAMED OF

Janet Snow
HAIR COLOR SPECIALIST

BURGESS SALON IN THE NORTH MALL
CALL 555-1256
FREE CONSULTATION • TRY ON A CHANGE OF COLOR

FIGURE 1-3 Business card offering a free consultation

"dream" of what their color could look like! Clients who may not be quite ready for a change in color, but have toyed with the idea or are just starting to get gray, may become brave enough to make a change. Because this card offers a free try on consultation, it will be an inspiration to some clients to be a little daring and "try" you as a hair colorist.

You may want to use the salon logo on your cards, but be sure to check with the salon manager before doing so. Using the salon logo may help to create interest in your work because the salon logo will bring the salon's reputation to the mind of potential clients. Logos can become universal trademarks; just think of a pair of jeans with a patch and a "W" on the leather patch on a back pocket and only one name comes to mind—Wrangler™.

Be creative and put some thought into your choices! This card will represent you and bring you

clientele. Be sure it reflects the image you really want to portray!

TEAMWORK

The next area that you will want to concentrate on is *teamwork*. By teaming up with other stylists, nail technicians, and estheticians you can take advantage of a network of professional people who already know your work and are ready to suggest your name to potential clients—you are gaining **referrals**.

• Other stylists in your salon may not have time to take new clients or may not want to do a certain type of work that you do wonderfully!

• Other stylists may also refer their overbookings and overflow clients to you, if you have met with them and you both have agreed on an arrangement to assist them in this manner. Perhaps they may refer all color services, braiding, or perms to you, or all appointments that must be made on their day off or vacation time could be booked with you. They will probably welcome the help and you will have clients to work on while you build your clientele.

Don't forget that every time you do another stylist's clients, you send out a walking ad of your work. Do your best work on these team client referrals and watch your own clientele build!

- Nail technicians and estheticians will also refer clients to you, if you meet with them and explain that you would like to give their clients a special service because they were referred by them. Perhaps you could offer a special discount for same-day bookings with both of you. Be sure to return the favor and refer your clients to them.

- Stylists, nail technicians, and estheticians from other salons may even want to try a "team referral" with you. Every salon has days when it is booked to the maximum and staff would love to suggest an alternative to disappointing a client.

- Perhaps one of your fellow beauty school students could team up with you.

- You could even contact all your former beauty school classmates, have a mini-reunion, and suggest the teamwork concept!

- The more people you put on your team, the faster you will build your clientele! Even friends, current clients, family, and neighbors can be on your team and help you by giving out your business cards and referring clients to you.

- Offer family and friends an incentive to help by giving them discount services or free services for three or more referrals. (More about this in Chapter 4.)

As you choose promotions from this book, try the teamwork approach and invite others to join you in the promotion. Promotions create interest and excitement in the salon, and they can be fun! The more people involved in the promotion, the better the exposure for you and the salon and the more successful the promotion will be!

Summary

- New salons must promote themselves to build a strong clientele, quickly.
- Be sure your image fits in with the salon image. It may be time for a makeover!
- Exposure through promotions will help reveal your talents and services to potential clients.
- The more promotions you do, the more exposure you will receive and the faster you will build a clientele!

- Special business cards and flyers will help new stylists become successful, faster!
- Use logos and discounts on your business cards!
- Teamwork with other stylists can make your promotions more successful and fun.
- Teamwork referrals can help you broaden your base for potential new clients.
- Everyone can be part of your team and help you with referrals. Include family, friends, current clients, and neighbors.

Key Terms Defined

Exposure: This occurs when you use promotions to present yourself to the community as a stylist who is ready to accept and service new clients. Potential customers become aware of who you are and what you have to offer them.

Professional Courtesy: When you receive or give a free service to another stylist, it is a professional courtesy.

Referrals: These are customers who have been sent to you by someone else. Someone has suggested to this client that you would be their perfect stylist!

Salon Image: The way your salon portrays itself to clients. The salon image is a facsimile of all the salon employees as well as the salon itself. The image you project is a representation of who you are and what you have to offer. Your behavior and dress are part of both the salon's image and yours!

Transient Trade: Clients who walk into the salon or call for an appointment, for the first time, and do not request a specific stylist, are called transient trade. They are looking for a new stylist and some new ideas. Promotions will bring many transient clients to the salon.

know your market

WHO ARE YOUR SALON'S CLIENTS?

Before you can conduct a successful promotion, you will need to decide exactly which clients you are trying to reach. This **client base** is also called your **market**. Once you decide on which group of clients or market you wish to target, you can choose a promotion that will entice those clients to try your salon. Promotions that work in one market may not work in another, so it is important to make this decision before you spend time or money on a promotion.

Just as there are many types of salons and many types of stylists and technicians in the beauty industry, there are many types of clients you may wish to add to your client base. A successful promotion will attract the right client for your salon and for the right stylist.

UPSCALE/PROFESSIONAL SALONS

Some salons are upscale and posh. They have a quiet atmosphere and a often a plush interior. They frequently offer a complete array of beauty services and they excel in pampering the client! Prices in these salons are usually a bit higher than average. This type of upscale salon would have mostly "professional" people as their market and would choose promotions that would appeal to this client.

- This salon may wish to do a promotion that offers discounts to doctors and nurses and send a flyer to the local medical college or hospital for their bulletin board (Figure 2-1).

- Perhaps they would like to do a promotion that would offer professional patrons the privilege to come in for early-morning appointments on their way to the office or they may provide lunchtime specials with quick *"in & out"* appointments.

- They may give country club members a special price for a certain service on the day they play golf, tennis, or racquetball.

- Promotions aimed at spouses can work well in this salon, too! This salon might try offering the spouse a half-price gift certificate for any one service when the spouse joins

Call for
your appointment
today—

919-555-1212

CITY SALON

Offers Nurses: Two for One Discount!

Any Monday during the month of January, nurses are welcome to car pool to our salon and split the cost of your perm with a co-worker, when you both have our deluxe body wave!

10 Elms Court Shopping Center
Mayville

FIGURE 2-1 Flyer for a nurse discount

FIGURE 2-2 Half-price coupon for a client's spouse

the current customer on the next appointment (Figure 2-2).

- Because good use of time is important to a professional person, this salon would probably offer punctuality and impeccable scheduling. This promise should be promoted in the brochure.

- The salon may also provide cellular phones, hookups for laptop computers, and a fax machine for the professional client to use. Of course, the salon would want to promote these amenities as a reason to frequent this salon!

- Some upscale salons have day spas and may wish to use promotions that advertise that business. Day spas are "mini salons" inside the salon, which offer massages and specialty skin care packages. It is like going to an exclusive health spa for the day!

- Above all, promotions for the upscale or professional salon must be subtle and tasteful. A room full of balloons and a clown would not work in this salon, but a room full of flowers that will be given to each woman on the Saturday before Mother's Day would be a smash hit!

MIDDLE-INCOME SALONS

Clients in a middle-income bracket will probably be the largest segment of the population in your city. Persons earning an average income, living in traditional housing, and having a family will usually fall into this category. To reach this market of middle-income clients, you must:

- give them quality services at a moderate price;
- offer sales they can take advantage of;
- offer the latest styles that you see on television, in movies, and on videos.

••••••••••••••••••••••••••••••••••••••

This is the clientele that wore the "Farah Fawcett" style, the "Dorothy Hamill" haircut, the "Princess Di" look, and the "Rachel shag" haircut from the *Friends* television program. They are looking for trends, current styles, and good prices.

••••••••••••••••••••••••••••••••••••••

When considering promotions for this market:

- You may wish to include a family special that offers mom, dad, and the children a special rate for haircuts if they all come in during the same week.
- You may even wish to make this a month-long promotion for a slow month, like July.

A simple flyer (Figure 2-3) that you can distribute to nursery schools and neighborhood schools would be all you need!

Another promotion that works well for middle-income clients is called "Makeover Magic."

If you do not have a full-service salon that offers makeovers, team up with a local makeup artist or a cosmetic salesperson and offer a day of makeovers. For a small fee, you will give clients a new style, the makeup person will accentuate the positive for them, and you can even offer them a photo session if someone in your salon is good with a camera! Perhaps a photographer in the area would offer a free 5x7 photo in hopes of selling a whole package of photos.

Everyone has fun at these photo shoots and you will make many new clients. Just picture that photo on your client's wall and every time someone asks her (or him) about it, your salon is mentioned. A small newspaper ad or a flyer given out in the salon or through a mailing list is all you need for this promo. It really sells itself!

Mailing Lists. A great way to make a mailing list for your salon is to have a drawing for a free makeover. Ask clients to place the name of someone they would like to treat to a makeover in the drawing box. If their friend is chosen, they win, too! Let clients enter every time they come in the salon and soon your box will be bulging with names of people who need your tender loving care!

Sports Menu. Another promotion that reaches middle-income clients is a sports menu. Simply list a sport term and name a service after it (Figure 2-4). List the special prices

before you head to the beach...

bring your head to us

family discount days!

When all of the family has haircuts on the same day—

pay just half price for all of your haircuts!

Kim's Salon
555-1215

FIGURE 2-3 Flyer for family promotion

LIZ'S SALON

Introduces
SPRING TRAINING
for Your Hair & Nails

Tennis Manicures
  for a comfortable grip $12.00
Golf Haircut
  a swinging bob $15.00
Runners Pedicure
  soothe those tired puppies $15.00
Aerobic Perm
  all the bounce you'll ever need $50.00

Present your
SPORTS CARD MEMBERSHIP
to take advantage
of these
SPECIAL PRICES

LIZ'S
121 Main Road
555-1234

LIZ'S NORTH
445 Tenth Street
555-4321

FIGURE 2-4 Sports menu promotion

and distribute a flyer to health clubs and fitness centers.

Team Up With a Boutique. For sure-fired results in a promotion for the middle-income client, team up with a local clothing boutique or specialty store.

- Ask the store to put on a fashion show and you will do the hair and nails for the models.

- Volunteer to put this promotion on for a local church or PTA. Use the members of the organization for models and watch your clientele grow!

- Both your salon and the clothing store should swap flyers and stuff bags with them and post them in your businesses.

- You can even include a shoe store in the fashion show and expand your bag stuffer distribution.

Value-Priced Salons

Value-priced salons attract a special type of client. These clients shop at the discount stores and usually are looking for value-priced services from a reputable salon.

• •

Value pricing happens when the same item or service is available in two salons and one salon provides it for a lower price. In the past these customers were called "Bargain Hunters;" now they have been tagged the "*Value-Priced* Shoppers!"

• •

Borrow An Idea From Successful Salons!

- *Never* let a bag full of retail items leave *your own salon* without *your flyer* in it. Flyers cost pennies and if you make them the type that children can color and put up on the refrigerator at home, you will have free advertising in their home, all week long!

- To make a flyer that children can color in, simply put cute graphics on it and print it on white paper (Figure 2-5). Make a note on the bottom that suggests the young artist may color it and bring it in for a prize next month. Give out a pencil with the salon name on it for a prize to every child who enters. Parents like their children to be recognized for their efforts!

The best way to reach the price-driven client is to have a price menu on a sign or a blackboard at the salon entrance.

- List three or four basic services and prices and make no substitutes.

- Offer clients good work at a very low price, but include no frills.

- Clients are served on a walk-in basis so appointments are not needed.

Kids Cuts Half Price

July 5th Only

Michael's Salon
666-1234

 COLOR THIS FLYER AND WIN A PRIZE

FIGURE 2-5 Flyer for children to color

- For example, you may offer a menu like this:

  Haircuts $10

  Blow-dry style $5

  Perms $30

  Conditioners $2

This type of basic work is quick and easy and you make your money in volume. A small newspaper ad or flyers passed out at local factories, hospitals, and cafeterias should be all the promotion that you would need. Be sure to mention the fact that appointments are not needed and children are welcome. List the salon hours in the flyer. You may want to consider that some shift workers need after-hours appointments.

Specialty Salons

Many salons are full-service salons that offer multiple services under one roof. Other salons, however, are *specialty salons* and offer only one service that they specialize in.

• •

A specialty salon may only offer hair services, or it may only offer nail services. There are even salons that offer skin care services only. When you choose just one type of service and only offer that one service, you are a specialist!

• •

These salons would use promotions to promote only the services they provide. For example, a salon that provides services in haircuts only would use promotions that apply only to haircuts. Many generic promotions can be tailored to fit a specialty salon. You may see a promotion in Chapter 10, which was designed for a "haircut sale," but your salon specializes in skin care only. You can take the same promotion designed for haircuts and alter it to use for facials (Figures 2-6 and 2-7). For example:

SNOWMAN SPECIAL

TWO family members get haircuts for the price of **ONE**...

...on any day it snows!

Walk-ins only

JOHNATHON'S SALON

675-1232

FIGURE 2-6 Promotion for "Two Haircuts for the Price of One"

This promotion for haircuts offers "Two Haircuts for the Price of One" when family members have a haircut at the same time. If you like the concept, change the wording in the sale flyer and give your customers "Two Facials for the Price of One."

SNOWMAN SPECIAL

TWO family members get facials for the price of **ONE**...
...on any day it snows!

Walk-ins only

JOHNATHON'S SALON
675-1232

FIGURE 2-7 Wording changed to "Two Facials for the Price of One"

Men Only Salons. Other salons offer services only to a certain segment of the population. For example, some salons are for gentlemen only! These salons may offer:

- oversized chairs
- sports decor
- sports videos playing in the waiting area
- a very masculine menu of services

Be creative and set up a menu of services named for sports stars. For example: "The Mickey Mantle Haircut"—a longer length style that is a sure hit every time at bat! "The Andre Agassi Haircut"—when you are ready for a total change to short hair!

Some men's salons offer early-morning and late-evening appointments to accommodate men who work long hours. They may even offer take-out service food delivered to them while they are having a pedicure or color service. (Team up with a local sub shop on this one!)

Whatever promotions you choose for this salon, be sure they are masculine and in good taste!

Children's Salons. Some salons provide services for children only! The salon may use smaller furniture and have cartoons playing on televisions scattered throughout the salon. The entire staff and salon are geared to the needs of children. This salon would chose promotions to appeal to youngsters, and to the parents of potential clients.

- Give away toys (trinkets, like the fast food chains do).
- Have drawings for amusement park tickets.
- Have a clown outside to hand out balloons to children as they enter the door. (Of course, the salon name is on the balloons!)

- Make up retail packages of no-tears shampoos and conditioners.

- Have stickers made with the salon name and number on it and decorate every retail bottle with a sticker before it leaves the children's salon!

- Package all retail bottles in a mesh bag the children can take into the tub to store water toys in. Put your name on the bag that can hang on the faucets and lets wet toys drip in the tub. Parents will love the mesh bag and for pennies you will have your name in front of them, daily.

Promotions for this salon can be the most fun of all! Just think of what would make a child happy and offer it!

- Try ice cream coupons that are punched for each haircut and redeemable from a neighborhood ice cream parlor.

- Try the same promotion with McDonalds™ 50¢ gift certificates.

You may even wish to try a tee-shirt promotion (see Chapter 10).

Teenage Salons. Other salons concentrate on teen clients only! The latest music playing, the latest clothes on the salon's staff, and the latest trends in hairstyles are the order for the day in this salon! Salons that specialize in children or teen services must do research to keep on top of current **trends** in what appeals

to the young! If you are unsure what appeals to them, ask a child or teen!

A word of caution: trends change daily, so do not invest a lot of money in a long-term promotion for teen salons. Try lots of small promotions with small investments until you are sure what works!

Salons for Older Adults. Another type of salon that seems to be popping up everywhere is one geared to older clients. As baby boomers age, there are more older adults than ever before. Salons specializing in this clientele offer a slow pace and a quiet atmosphere. Promotions for this salon could include:

- early-bird discounts for appointments before 10 AM;

- a special on perms for hard-to-curl gray hair;

- give-aways of shampoo that takes the yellow out of gray hair; be sure your salon sticker is on the bottle.

Promotions that create nostalgia are winners in this salon. For example, try a photo contest. Have clients bring in photos of beehive hairstyles they wore in the 1960s, hang them up on a bulletin board with numbers under them, and have all the clients vote for the one they like the best (Figure 2-8). Give away a free style as a prize and watch the fun unveil as the old photos come out of the albums!

FIGURE 2-8 Promotion for salon catering to older adults

The perfect place to promote yourself with seniors is at the local senior centers, churches, and retirement communities. Check your local telephone directory for listings in your city.

Summary

> Know who your salon's clients are before you choose a promotion.
> Some salons have only upscale clients and should use subtle promotions.
> Salons with middle-income clients should provide family offers and trendy promotions.
> Value-priced clients want a good service at a good price, with no frills involved.
> Specialty salons include one service only salons, men's salons, children or teens only salons, and salons for older clients.
> Specialized clientele require specialized promotions.

Key Terms Defined

Client Base: The group of clients you wish to attract. A client base can be made up of any group of people with a common need. For example, you may choose a client base that consists of children only.

Market: The term market in this chapter means the exact same thing as client base. Your market will be the group of people you wish to service in your salon, for example, middle-income clients.

Trend: The inclination or direction things are moving toward. A former trend in hairstyling was to spiral perm long hair and let it dry naturally into a curly style.

Value Pricing: Same item or service offered in two salons and one salon provides it for a lower price. When customers look for a good, basic, no-frills service at a very affordable price, they are considered value-priced shoppers. These clients were formerly called bargain hunters.

preparing for salon promotions

IN THIS CHAPTER, YOU WILL LEARN:

- How to prepare yourself, and your salon, for promotions
- Importance of salon appearance
- How to decide on the salon's potential
- The importance of a business plan
- How to choose a mission statement
- How to motivate other staff members
- The purpose of a salon brochure

KEY TERMS

- brand recognition
- customer service
- mission statement

APPEARANCE AND POTENTIAL

Before you can successfully promote yourself and your salon, you must prepare as though you were getting yourself ready to meet the most distinguished client in the world. If you always think of every client who comes into your salon as royalty, you will be prepared to succeed.

As we learned in Chapter 1, every salon has an image and every stylist in the salon should portray that image. All stylists must make an exceptionally good impression on clients by being neat, clean, and impeccably manicured and coifed. It is amazing how much emphasis a client will put on your appearance. Potential clients will choose a stylist who wears a style they would like to have or has an image or "look" that they are trying to achieve. Therefore, one of the best promotions you can do to help yourself is to be sure you represent the positive side of cosmetology at all times.

• •

Be sure your hairstyle is flattering, your color is freshly retouched, and your nails are neatly manicured. You may want to trade services with another staff member to be sure that you always look your best.

• •

Salon Appearance

Part of presenting a good image to clients is preparing the salon's appearance! You may not have the finances to change the decor in the salon, but everyone in the salon can work on salon appearance.

Every salon must be kept neat, impeccably clean, and in good order, at all times!

First impressions are lasting impressions and you may not be able to change the image clients get when they walk through the door and your salon looks less than attractive.

- The reception area and waiting room must be straightened every morning and checked throughout the day! This area must never be in disarray because this is the first area your clients will see. Throw out outdated or tattered magazines, keep clutter to a minimum, and be sure the wastebaskets and ashtrays are emptied throughout the day.
- Be certain retail displays are immaculate and filled to capacity.

- Be sure everything in the dressing room is clean (including the mirror) and that it is well stocked with robes for clients having chemical services.
- There should be a hamper for clients to dispose of soiled robes and a rack for their clothes. Be sure to check this area often.
- Shampoo areas and workstations should always be kept neat and clean.
- Hair should be swept up immediately and placed in a closed container. It should never be left on the floor while you style the hair; it poses a hazard and hair scatters all over the room as it dries.
- Be a good team player and sweep for other stylists when you are not busy. The stylists will appreciate it and clients will notice it, too.
- Be sure the back bar of the shampoo area is well stocked every morning.
- Preparation is the key to success! You will find it easier to work if everything you need is at your fingertips and you do not have to leave a client once you have started the service.

There is no substitute for a clean, organized salon. Clients will notice and respond to your efforts.

Customer Service

An important part of salon image is the way that you treat customers.

The salon should have a **customer service** policy that is always strictly followed.

••••••••••••••••••••••••••••••••••

Everything you do or say should reflect the fact that you care about your clients and their requirements. From the music the salon plays to the greeting on the telephone, you must consider the client's needs above everything else.

••••••••••••••••••••••••••••••••••

Everyone in the salon should make the customer's needs the top priority.

- Clients should receive your undivided attention and be made to feel comfortable in your salon.

- From the moment you greet clients until the time they leave the salon, you are on stage and they are observing everything you say and do.

- Treat every client as though he or she is a welcomed and honored guest.

- Keep a professional attitude and a customer-centered outlook so that you will be a success with new clients.

- Customer complaints and concerns should always be handled as quickly and as quietly as possible. It is unrealistic to think that you are going to please every customer you ever do, so if a client is unhappy, be sure that the person is redone or

> ### Borrow An Idea From an Expert Stylist!
>
> 🖉 Milady offers a wonderful book, *Keep 'em Coming Back: SalonOvations' Guide to Salon Promotion and Client Retention,* by Lee Hoffman. The chapter on salon image is a marvelous tool to help you learn to give your clients impeccable service and put forth a positive salon image.

given a refund as quickly and as pleasantly as possible. Always remember that other clients are watching you handle tough situations, so be polite and courteous at all times!

A satisfied customer will tell two or three friends about your salon, but unhappy customers will tell everyone they meet!

Salon Potential

Every salon has a potential that is unique! To achieve success as a stylist, you must realize the potential of your salon and take advantage of it when building your own following. For example, if your salon only offers haircutting, but you are an expert in perms and colors, do research to see if the salon has the potential to add these services to the menu.

Concentrate on the opportunities available in the salon but that have been an untapped area until now. If you enjoy giving manicures as well as hair services, perhaps you could offer them to clients already coming to the salon for hair services.

Take advantage of other stylists' talents and learn from them. Ask them questions and you will benefit from the wealth of experience and knowledge that is at your fingertips.

Be sure to discuss salon potential with the staff and be certain you fully understand both the potential and the capacity for salon growth (both of which will directly affect your following).

••••••••••••••••••••••••••••••••••••

A salon that has reached its maximum potential will be busy at all times and you will find it easy to build a personal clientele in this environment. A salon that is new or has not yet reached its potential has many undiscovered resources that could be a potential niche for you to fill. You may have to work hard to find those niches and reach your potential, but the reward will be your satisfied clientele. Communicate with the salon staff and uncover the salon's potential!

••••••••••••••••••••••••••••••••••••

You will want to take continuing education classes, so that you are always reaching your potential, too. Try to attend as many trade shows as you can. Attend seminars and classes as they are offered in your area. Your local beauty supply company can be a good resource for continuing education classes.

YOUR BUSINESS PLAN

Every business should have a business plan. Your business plan is the strategy you will use to achieve your financial goals. When you decide how much money the salon will earn in total sales each month, you must set up a plan to decide what percentage of the income will be used for promotions. This figure is called your *promotional (advertising) budget.* To determine your salon's business plan, you may want to have an accountant help you set up a system, or you may let your local office of SCORE (Service Corps of Retired Executives) help you decide on a business plan. SCORE is a government office of volunteers who have run successful businesses, and they are ready and willing to help you with your business plan, free of charge.

In your business plan, you may want to include your financial plans, promotional plans, current finances, business projections, plans for expansion, and potential for growth. There are also many good books on the subject of business plans. Check the local library and community colleges. Sometimes classes on small businesses are held at your local community college; these will help you learn how to write a small business plan.

New businesses and new stylists will want to spend more money on promotions than established businesses, but everyone must advertise to remain successful! When you are just beginning your business you will want to spend money on more promotions, which will help you *capture* the market. When you capture the market, you gain **brand recognition**.

In Chapter 1, we learned that some companies have such strong brand recognition they have captured their market and their name is synonymous with the product (e.g., Kleenex and Polaroid™).

Your goal is to achieve brand recognition for your salon (and you personally) just like Vidal Sassoon™ and Paul Mitchell™ have. Brands are either successful or fail on the strength of advertising and promotions.

- You can be the world's best stylist, but if you do not promote yourself and gain brand recognition, who will know how wonderful you are?

- If you do not promote yourself and earn enough money to stay in business, who will ever see your talent?

SCENARIO

Ben and Chris' salon has a projected income of $100,000 for next year. They earned $80,000 last year, but they have added *one stylist* to the staff, and they expect that new stylist to bring in an additional $20,000 in sales. They have allocated 15% of their $100,000 revenue to promotions and advertising, so their new advertising budget is $15,000.

They have planned to spend the money in the following proportions:

MONTH	BUDGET	NOTED FROM LAST YEAR
January	$2,000	Cold weather—business slow
February	1,000	Business picked up
March	800	Business great—Easter
April	1,200	Rainy weather—business slow
May	500	Proms kept us booked to capacity
June	2,000	June good, prepare for dead July
July	2,000	July—heat wave killed business
August	500	Good month
September	500	Back-to-school sales helped
October	1,000	Good month—started holiday promos
November	2,000	Good month—focused on Xmas promos
December	1,500	Good month—start Jan. promos now

All stylists are a product, but you are the *brand* of stylist you wish to promote (just as all tissues are a product but Kleenex is a *brand*). To build this brand recognition, you must have a plan and stick to it, as seen in the previous scenario.

- You will notice that they looked at the previous year's records and prepared notes and dollar amounts to reflect the business trends they had and are anticipating for this year.

- If they had a difficult January last year and several years before, it would make sense that they should plan on promotion for January sales by doing extra promotions in December and January.

- Notice that they do not plan to promote strongly in a month like May because they are always booked to capacity and June is traditionally good, too.

- If your salon does not have records yet, start saving the appointment books and making notes in the margin.

Keep track of the following items:

Salon income

New clients

Retail sales

Weather

Promotions

At the end of the week, total up all the days.

At the end of the month, total up all the weeks.

Once you have your budget, you can then decide on promotions you

WRITE THE MONTHLY TOTALS BELOW:

MONTH	INCOME	NOTED
January	$	
February		
March		
April		
May		
June		
July		
August		
September		
October		
November		
December		
YEARLY TOTALS:		

would like to do, depending on how much money you have to spend for that month. Your budget will vary depending on the size of your salon and the amount of money your salon grosses, but keep in mind that you can do a promotion for as little as $20, so there is a promotion for everyone in Chapter 10.

MISSION STATEMENT

Before you begin any promotions, you should decide on a **mission statement** for your salon. A mission statement is the written account of the goals you will be trying to achieve with your sales plan and promotions in the coming year. It is a declaration that describes:

1. what your salon really is
2. where your salon is going

It is the map to reach your goals.

Here is a simple mission statement for an upscale salon in the downtown area of a large city:

••

Gina Marie's Salon— Mission Statement 1997

To reach and retain clients in a consistent manner, the following items are included in our mission statement:

1. we will always put the client's needs above our own. If there is ever a conflict between the two, the customer's needs will always come first;
2. every aspect of our salon will be customer-centered and focused;

3. our salon has two primary goals: to offer the highest quality, customer-centered service at all times and to maintain a reputation in the community for being progressive trendsetters;

4. when this mission is accomplished, we will open a second salon on the west side of town.

••

You can see by this mission statement that the salon owners want to achieve impeccable customer service, a good reputation, and expansion to a second location. Now that they know where they are going, they can plan a yearly promotional calendar to help them get there.

STAFF TRAINING AND MOTIVATION

The entire salon staff must be trained to be successful at promotions. It is imperative that a salon meeting be held during which everyone is allowed to brainstorm promotional ideas and plan promotions.

••

Be sure everyone understands all the terms of the promotion and how it will work. One weak link can cause the entire promotion to fail!

••

Give out handouts that tell how, when, where, and why the promotion is being held. Be sure all involved understand their part in the promotion.

CONTEST CONTEST CONTEST CONTEST CONTEST CONTEST

During the spring haircolor sale, April 10th through 15th, perform the most color services and win a dinner at West's!

	MARY	SUE	LINDA	MIKE	PETER
April 10:	2	1	0	5	1
April 11:	1	1	1	1	2
April 12:	5	2	0	4	4
April 13:	0	4	4	1	1
April 14:	0	2	6	1	2
April 15:	2	2	2	0	0
TOTALS:	10	12	13	12	10

(Post a simple chart like this in the dispensary and watch all the stylists get competitive and try harder to sell color services!)

Contests

The best way to get everyone involved is to set up a friendly competition or contest!

An example of a contest could be as simple as the chart shown above.

Staff Pictures and Videos

One of the most exciting promotions you can do is to take a staff photo or make a staff video. Everyone in the salon will get excited over this idea! A staff portrait can be placed in the window, in the waiting area, in newspaper ads, flyers, on business cards, and in your communication to clients. People will remember a face longer than a name, so put the faces of your salon staff on display.

A staff video can be useful for promotional purposes, too.

Borrow an Idea From a Successful Salon

- One of the nicest salon photos you can create is a photo of all of you holding your scissors up.

- Or, if the staff is small, all of the staff can be styling one client's hair! Be creative and imaginative and have fun with the photo. Be sure everyone's hair and nails are impeccable for the portrait—you may even want to wear similar colors when you take the photo (all wear black slacks and red tops or all wear blue shirts and ties).

- You can run the video in the waiting room at all times.

- You can send it for promotions outside of the salon.

- Perhaps a neighborhood dress shop would exchange videos with you and you could run them for each other!

Be sure the video shows all the staff members doing their best work and shows the salon in the best light! Try to make the video as enticing as you can; put yourself in a client's shoes and walk through the salon with the camera rolling! You will be surprised at what you see! Be sure the video is done when everything is polished and clean and ready for royalty. Scrutinize the video before you show it to clients. Be tough on yourself when you review the video—put your best foot forward or do not use it.

Brochures

Brochures and pamphlets are the oldest form of advertising! They are inexpensive and they work, if you do them right. A few rules must be followed when making brochures:

1. your message always goes on the cover. Think of it as a headline that tells the world who and what you are! Use a single illustration on the cover;

Borrow an Idea From the Best

📖 Pick up brochures from your neighborhood hotels, restaurants, tourist centers, and clubs. Compare them and borrow ideas or concepts that you like. Use the ideas that catch your eye and make you want to try their business!

2. do not get too fancy and do not clutter it up with a lot of little pictures...less is more;

3. keep it simple and try to make only one point with the brochure;

4. use good quality paper, printing, and photography or illustrations; this is not an area to scrimp;

5. use captions under all photos;

6. put a calendar or a list of special events on the back, make it something the client will want to keep or even post on the refrigerator.

Have fun creating a brochure that you will be able to mail to new people in your town, hand out at parades and fairs, and distribute to every civic club in the area. The possibilities are endless!

Summary

- Prepare for promotions by working on salon image, appearance, and potential.
- Know the salon's potential before you begin a promotion.
- Every salon must have a business plan.
- A mission statement is a report or a statement that tells what the salon wants to achieve.
- Staff training is important to promotional success.
- Competition makes promotions fun and more successful.
- Staff pictures and videos bring your staff to the attention of your potential clients.
- Brochures are a brief overview and an invitation to visit your salon.

Key Terms Defined

Brand Recognition: The name of a particular brand of product that has been promoted so successfully that the product's name is now synonymous with the product.

Customer Service: This is the manner in which you service customers. Good customer service means that you are putting the customer's needs before anything else, every time the client enters your salon.

Mission Statement: One or two ideas that relate what you would like your salon to achieve and how you plan to reach that goal.

courting current clients and retaining them

IN THIS CHAPTER, YOU WILL LEARN:

- How to *retain your current clients* for a lifetime
- How to *maintain client records* to enhance repeat business
- The importance of *tracking sales*
- The most productive ways to handle *client concerns*
- How to *listen for client needs*
- Which *promotions* are for existing clients only
- Why you should *introduce new services to current clients*

KEY TERMS

- client concerns
- tracking sales
- vision

A CLIENT–STYLIST RELATIONSHIP is a love affair that is meant to last a lifetime! However, just like any other relationship, you must work at keeping alive the interest that drew the customer to you in the first place. When you were first trying to build your clientele, you made a special effort to catch the eye of your current clients. You pampered them and gave them sales, specials, coupons, and the latest styles. To keep these clients, you must continue to "court" them and keep them excited about you and what you have to offer. If all of your promotions offer sales and "perks" to only new clients, your current clients may start to feel that you take them for granted and look for another stylist who is ready and willing to "pursue" them.

CUSTOMER APPRECIATION

Let your customers know that you appreciate their business! Many of

...s in Chapter 10 can be ...ent clients, but some... ...I want to offer special little gestures like these to keep a client "in love" with you.

- Send thank you notes when they refer a client! Include a coupon for a free trim in the note.
- Send birthday cards to all of your clients.
- On the week preceding Mother's Day, pass out one long-stem rose to every woman who comes in that week. (You can buy roses in bulk at a local florist supply or greenhouse —if your budget is tight, carnations and daisies will work, too.)
- Cut out newspaper articles of your client's winning tennis match, her child's Little League score and her husbands' promotion. Tape the article to the mirror the day your client is scheduled to come in and watch her light up when she sees you are giving her recognition for an accomplishment. Everyone likes to feel like a star.
- Hold a "Customer Appreciation Day" and give clients 1% off for every year that they have been your client! Use client record cards to verify dates and discount percentages.
- Send out invitations and decorate the salon with an anniversary theme. Serve refreshments and give

out prizes. (Figure 4-1 offers a sample invitation.)

- Give out thank you gifts at Hanukkah and Christmas.
- Key chains with your salon name on them are a great thank you gift.
- Rain bonnets and nail files with your salon logo are great, too.
- Have a discount tree with little balloons on it. Slip a piece of paper into the balloon and list a discount on it. Let clients pop the balloons with a pin and reap the discount they choose at random!

Salon Greensboro

Extends a Special Invitation to Our Honored Clients!

Allow us to celebrate your loyal patronage by attending our

Open House
and
Customer Appreciation Day Celebration

Prizes, Refreshments, and Fun will Abound!

Drop by and Bring a Friend!

May 10, 1997 8am to 9pm

FIGURE 4-1 Invitation to a salon customer appreciation day

CLIENT REFERRAL CARDS

For referrals, offer your current clients your business cards to distribute. Tell clients to sign the back of the cards and give them to friends. When three of the cards are turned in by friends who come in for a service, you will give the client a free haircut! When six are turned in, you will give her a free perm.

Be sure to keep accurate records; perhaps you can staple the cards to your client's record card.

CLIENT RECORDS

When a client comes in for a service, you should take a moment to write on the back of the record card what you discussed that day. In addition to her service, you probably talked about a new style, a new retail item, her golf match this month, her mother's visit, and her daughter's dance recital.

When you see the client's name on the book next week or next month, take a moment to review her card for what you did for a service and what you talked about concerning her life! Everyone needs to feel special, so if you greet her with a question like "Mrs. Andrews, how did your son's last soccer game turn out?" or "Mr. Gold, I remember your mother is coming to visit this week; here is a discount coupon for her, we

Take a Tip From the Top

🖋 Send a note that says, "We miss you," when any client is away on vacation, has not been in for a month, or misses an appointment. Just a simple, preprinted postcard will do!

would love to give her a half-price manicure while she is here" or "Ms. Jepson, I remember that your garden club was going on a trip to Savannah, did you have fun? How did your new hairstyle do? Was it easy to maintain while you traveled?"

....

The best promotion is really caring about your client's needs.

....

TRACKING SERVICE AND PRODUCT SALES

By **tracking sales** and services, you will be aware of which services are not being taken advantage of and which retail items need to be introduced through a promotion or a sale.

• On your appointment book, each week, add up the color, perm, relaxer, haircut, skin, and nail services you did. Total each category for the month and you will see a trend developing!

	WEEK 1	WEEK 2	WEEK 3	WEEK 4	MONTH TOTALS
Perms					
Cuts					
Colors					
Relaxers					
Styles					
Manicures					
Pedicures					

- If perm sales are sagging, try a promotion specifically for perms. In Chapter 8, there is a "one-day perm sale" that is sure to do the trick.

- If haircuts are your least selling service, try a cut-a-thon or hot haircut promo. (Chapter 10 has several ideas to sell cuts to new and existing clients.)

- Keep both retail sales records and inventories of each item. If you see an item has never sold very well, perhaps the staff does not like it, or they do not understand how to use it properly…so they never recommend it. Have a staff meeting and decide if the product is a good one and how to promote it. At the meeting, decide if you need:

1. a better retail display

2. a training class for stylists to learn about the product

3. a sale or discount to introduce the item

4. a clearance sale to make way for a product that sells better

CLIENT CONCERNS

To keep the clients you have, you must stay in tune to client needs and **client concerns.**

Client needs and concerns may include:

1. complaints—not every client is going to like every service you provide;

2. fears—the client wants to try something new and needs to be reassured before she tries it;

3. complacency—she has worn this style for 10 years and does not want to give it up;

4. time—this client may not have the extra time to spend in the salon or maintaining a new style at home.

Client concerns should always be addressed as quickly, quietly, and pleasantly as possible. If it is a concern for the client, it should be a priority to you.

The key to answering all of your client's concerns and fears is to really communicate with her!

Communication is an exchange of ideas. Be sure to really listen to her, repeat what she has said, and give her an honest answer.

• •

Honesty and compassion have no substitute and always add up to success.

• •

INTRODUCING NEW SERVICES

You do not always need to think of promotions as something you do to reach new clients. Some current clients may be ready to try additional services or new styles. In fact, if your client has been coming to you for years it is probably time for a change. If you do not recommend something new, some other stylist may and you will lose your client. Always suggest something to update or revamp her look, at least semiannually as the seasons change and she is changing her wardrobe.

- Suggest highlights or color services.
- Suggest the same style, only add a perm to it.
- Suggest several new cuts; have photos ready when you present the idea.
- Suggest bangs if it has been a while since she had any.
- Suggest growing out bangs if she has always worn them.

Be gracious if your client declines a change. You have planted a seed and someday, when she needs a lift, your idea will germinate in her mind and grow into an opportunity to serve her.

• •

A successful scenario: Change your style and color slightly every season and your clients will copy your trends!

• •

Always take the time to give your clients a free consultation before every service. *Really listen* to what she is telling you!

1. Did her hair stay in well with this style?

2. How would she wear her hair if money were no object?

3. What is her worst hair nightmare?

4. What one thing would she say she liked best about her last service with you?

5. Ask her to point out three styles in your latest style book that most represent the style she wants.

Take notes on the back of her service card while she is answering your questions.

Think over the answers and set up a service plan for this client. Plan what you will need to do over the next few services to achieve her **vision** of perfection.

Plan out her next perm, color, cut, and so on. Write the prescription down and send a copy with her.

You have just handed your client a vision, a goal, and a reason to keep coming back to you!

WHILE YOU ARE HERE—
Bad Weather Promotion

Print up copies of a note pad similar to this one

PUT THEM AT EVERY STATION AND THE FRONT DESK

Every time it snows or the weather causes clients to cancel appointments, whip out the pad and offer every client currently in the salon a chance to have a half-price service with the purchase of the services she is currently having.

· · ·

Because you have cancellations, you will have time to try new colors or styles!

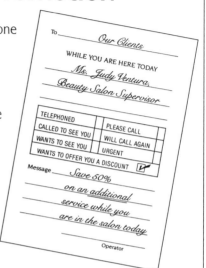

FIGURE 4-2 While you are here pad for promoting new services

Keep a pad in your desk—pull it out on rainy days, storm days, and slow days. Today, sell everyone a new service in addition to the one each had an appointment for! (The half-price offer inspires sales!)

Offer all the clients who come in today a sheet from the pad (Figure 4-2) and a sale that will fill up your appointment book.

Summary

- You must court and care for the customers you already have, while you are looking for new customers to add to your client base.
- Tracking services will help you learn where you need to concentrate your efforts and which services your current clients are not taking full advantage of.
- Really listen to your clients and take their concerns into consideration when they come into your salon each time.

- Appreciate current clients with special sales for them only and gifts and promotions that are geared toward their specific needs. Happy clients keep coming back and bring their friends with them.
- Keep up with all the important events in your client's life; it shows a genuine concern for her.

Key Terms Defined

Client Concerns: Anything that makes your customer unhappy, uneasy, or anxious, such as considering a new look, spending more time or money in your salon, or trying new retail items.

Tracking Sales: Keeping track of how many perms, cuts, colors, and so on you do each month. Look for areas that your customers are not fully using. Which services are you not promoting?

Vision: The picture you place in your client's mind when you suggest a new concept, look, or service to her. This is the mental image she has of her ideal look! Vision also means having the foresight to see things as they might become!

media advertising

IN THIS CHAPTER, YOU WILL LEARN:

▶ The forms of communication *media* that you may use to advertise your business

▶ How to choose an *advertising agency*

▶ What *print ads* are and how to use them

▶ How *radio and TV advertising* works

▶ What *on-line promotions* are

▶ How to use *coupons, flyers, and point of sale* pieces

KEY TERMS

▶ circulation

▶ collateral

▶ on-line promotions

▶ penetrate the market

▶ point of sale (POS)

THE MEDIA are the methods, processes, or vehicles that you, as a new stylist, will use to promote yourself and your business. Whether you hire an advertising agency to help you promote your business or handle the job yourself, you will need to be aware of the types of media available to make yourself known to the public. Everyone is familiar with radio, television, magazine, and newspaper advertising, but you may not be aware that there are other media you can use to promote yourself. In this chapter, we look at many other media choices and how they work.

Whichever media you choose, pick a concept or an idea that best describes you and use it consistently in all your ads and promotions. Use the same theme in all your ads and you will create a household name out of your salon's name.

••••••••••••••••••••••••••••••••••••

Penetration: When you **penetrate the market,** you use several media at once to reach a variety of clients. Using newspaper, radio, and flyers for the same perm sale penetrates the market and creates a campaign of advertising that promotes you in your community.

••••••••••••••••••••••••••••••••••••

ADVERTISING AGENCIES

Advertising agencies are firms that specialize in promoting your business. When an agency represents you, its staff evaluates your advertising needs and comes up with a *campaign* of suggestions, ideas, and concepts on how you can best promote your business. When you are choosing an advertising agency to promote your business, there are some key things to consider.

- Size of the agency. It should be small enough to need your business, but big enough to have other clients and experience in advertising for the cosmetology profession. What does the agency's portfolio look like? (Their portfolio is a collection of successful promotions they have recently accomplished.)
- Conflicts. A conflict of interest occurs when an agency represents two or more of the same types of business. For example, if the agency you choose also handles the advertising for another salon in your city, are there different teams at the agency so that your ads are not

being handled by the same people? Is the agency able to protect your trade secrets? Does the agency have a good reputation? Who is on their client list? Will they give you a list of clients as references?

- Creative awards. Which creative awards has the agency won? Awards mean that they are recognized by their peers for creativity and successful work.
- Price. Is the agency willing to work within your budget? Can you afford an agency to do your advertising for you or will you need to do all the work yourself?

One area that you may wish to consider before you decide on using an agency is the scope of their training and creativity. Are they specialists in advertising?

- Agencies know how to present promotions to the public in ways that achieve the best results.
- Agencies know how to get the most results from the money you spend on promotions and ads.
- Agencies know how to build a promotional campaign that will tie together all your promotions to build brand recognition for your salon.

You may wish to review Chapter 1, where we learned that large companies use promotional campaigns to gain recognition for their product's name. This is sometimes called *brand recognition* because the series of promotions or ads have caused you to recognize the brand and the product as soon as you hear the brand name.

••

IN THE WINK OF AN EYE…"Doing business without advertising is like winking at a girl in the dark. You know what you are doing, but nobody else does."
Stuart Henderson Britt, *New York Herald-Tribune*, October 30, 1956.

••

TYPES OF MEDIA

Print Ads

Print ads are a popular choice among media. Print ads are used in newspapers and magazines.

Newspapers. There are many types of newspapers:

- large business newspapers (e.g., *New York Times*)—**circulation** worldwide

- city newspapers (e.g., *Providence Journal Bulletin*)—circulation primarily in a particular city or region

- small town or neighborhood newspapers (e.g., *Lexington County Local Newspaper*)—circulation in your town or neighborhood

- industry newspapers (e.g., *Nursing News*)—circulation to primarily nurses or a specific group

- weekly newspapers (e.g., *Tri City Times*)—circulation to a three town area

- sports newspapers (e.g., *Sporting News*)—circulation centered on seasonal sports fans

- school newspapers (e.g., *City College News*)—circulation to the faculty and student body

Choosing in which newspaper to advertise may depend on several factors. Two important considerations are the cost for advertising in the particular paper and their actual circulation. The *New York Times* or the *Miami Herald* may be too expensive for you, and they may not have the circulation you wish to target as your market. (You may wish to review Chapter 2, in which we learned about market or customer.)

Small city or town newspapers as well as weekly newspapers are more affordable and probably reach *your client* more often. Research a newspaper well before you commit to using it for your advertising. Ask to see the demographics: how many people they reach, which segment of the population they are targeting, and how this can help your salon. Know that they can reach your market, before you purchase an ad with them.

Magazines. As a new stylist, you may choose to use a print ad in a magazine. Just as there are local and national newspapers, there are magazines that circulate nationally as well as ones that are used in your locality. National magazine ads are very expensive and will not be a good choice for a new stylist on a moderate budget, but local business publications, hobby magazines, and ladies magazines may be an affordable alternative. Go to a magazine stand and buy a few local magazines. If you want to use one of them, call the editor at the telephone number on the bottom of the title page. You may even offer to write a beauty column in exchange for a free ad!

Setting Up a Print Ad. If you have decided to place an ad in print, you should call the newspaper or magazine and request an appointment with the sales representative. Once you decide on price and how often you will run the ad, the creative department will take over and design an ad for you (usually the price of designing the ad is included in the cost of running the ad). After several meetings and proofing the ideas they create, you will sign off (give your approval) and the ad will run.

There are a few simple guidelines to remember in print advertising:

- keep it simple and uncluttered;
- your illustration should draw the readers attention before the words do;
- photos are better choices than sketches and artwork;
- headlines should grab the reader (offer the reader a benefit);
- keep copy (words in the ad) simple, clear, and brief. Make copy easy to read;
- be different and adventurous, try things other stylists do not have in print yet. Be a trendsetter!

Press Releases

Press releases are materials in which you describe a special event or party that will be held in your salon (e.g., fashion show, charity function, etc.). Newspapers often print press releases without charge. Simply send a letter to the editor and explain the special event, the dates, the purpose, and your name and telephone number. If the newspaper has space, they always try to run press releases. Send a press release two or three times a year to each newspaper. (Special events in which a charity is the beneficiary always get a lot of free press.)

Outdoor Advertising

Billboards and signs are forms of outdoor advertising. Your salon sign is probably the most expensive advertising you will do in your first year. Use a professional sign company and their designers and ideas! Check for competitive prices; there are even instant sign companies in most big cities.

You may wish to consider:

- banners—plastic or cloth (reasonable price, for temporary use);

- magnetic signs—your salon logo that will stick to the side of your car and lift off easily when needed;

- billboards—outdoor signs (cost can be prohibitive, but it never hurts to call and ask; you may be able to rent a small billboard in the slow season). Look in the Yellow Pages under outdoor advertising;

- blimps, bustops, buses, trains, taxis, and bus-stop shelters—call the owners of the companies, and get a price quote. If the price is right, work with a sign company to create the ad. The owner may work with one particular company and can get you a great price.

· ·

Color you smart: When using outdoor advertising, use a lot of color, focus on one idea, and make it stand out!

· ·

Radio Ads

As a new stylist, you will want to choose a local radio station that targets an audience that is your potential customer. Before you sign a contract for radio ads, ask the station for the demographics of their audience and when they listen to the station. (These figures are made available through independent surveys.)

Radio stations can prepare and cut the ad for you. Ask them to play some ads they have recently produced and to present some ideas for your ads. Keep in mind the following rules as you listen to what they are offering you.

Radio ads should:

- talk to the listener on a one-to-one basis (talk to one person at a time);

- use music in the background (soothing and memorable);

- use holidays and seasons for your client to associate you with (Christmas sale);

- advertise specials and dated sales (today-only clearance sale);

- focus on only one idea at a time (haircut sale);

- make the clients "see it" with their ears.

Television Ads

Like radio and newspaper, you can either buy local or national air time in television. Television is the most expensive way to advertise. A mere 15-second ad for a large sporting event could cost a million dollars. Therefore, a new salon would most likely want to start with local television ads, if they can find a local station that offers affordable air time. Just like radio, the television station can help you create and produce a commercial. You will have to shop for the best price and you may want to watch all of the local stations and take notes on the local ads. Note who is doing the best job getting your attention and which station is most appealing to *your potential market*.

Rules for good television commercials:

1. give viewers a solution to their problems (tame your unruly hair with our perm)
2. give viewers information they need
3. entertain viewers (make it real, make it fun, make it live)
4. tell viewers they will benefit from your service (look younger)
5. keep it simple and uncluttered
6. connect all your commercials with one consistent theme, to build brand recognition
7. use testimonials to verify your claims
8. use sex appeal and humor (both sell)

• •

Be penny wise: Keep an eye on production costs; they can add up fast. Be sure the producers understand that they must stay within the agreed budget for the commercial. Get the agreement in writing.

• •

On-line Advertising

There is a whole new world of **on-line advertising** opportunities on the Internet. You can use wonderful new ways to promote your business on the Internet. For a small fee, you can have your own Web site or home page (your personal page on the Internet) created. (Some college students may even create your page free, as a class project—call the computer science department of your local college.)

When you have a Web site on the Internet, people can search and find your home page and read about the current sales you are offering, find out about your prices, services, hours, location, or any other information that you wish to add to your Web site. (The possibilities are endless.) Try a computer coupon for a free trim and give your net buddies a reason to try you!

• •

Surf the Internet and see what is going on. Many on-line services offer you 10 free hours of service to try their Internet connection service. Connect to one and "surf the net," which means to go from one item to the next at random and see what you discover on the Internet. Any computer store can show you how to connect to the Internet.

• •

OTHER ADVERTISING METHODS
Coupons and Mail Offers

Coupons and mail offers are one of the best promotion methods. Per customer that you will reach, these two media have the lowest cost and the best return for the money.

- Coupons in mail packs work very well.
- Companies listed in the Yellow Pages in your city will make and distribute the value pack coupons to your neighborhood for you.
- You can make your own coupons

and give them out to your clients or surrounding neighborhoods.

- Take any flyer idea in Chapter 10, add a coupon on the bottom, and you have created a winning concept!

- Customers keep coupons and toss out plain flyers, so use a coupon on as many flyers as you can.

- Coupons, flyers, mailers, sometimes called **collateral**, are the pieces of advertising that customers hold in their hands.

Point of Sale

Sometimes **point of sale (POS)** is called point of purchase (POP), but it means the same thing—putting a sign at the point where the customer makes a purchase. POS includes:

- sale signs (50% off)

- posters (lists of things on sale or services offered)

- display pictures (of your work or styles you would like to entice your client into trying)

••

WHAT'S UP? What is your client looking at when you are shampooing her hair? A bare ceiling, right? Why not tack up a sale sign for her to focus on while she is lying back at the shampoo bowl?

••

Photographs

Blow up the photos that you take and make posters to hang in your salon. You can use a photographer or do the photos yourself. Be sure the quality is good and the photo shows off your best work. Practice makes perfect and, in time, you will learn how to pose the models and use backgrounds to compliment your work. There are many good books on photography—check a few out of the library.

••

Follow in these footsteps! A hot new idea is coming onto the scene—*floor advertising!* Paint footsteps from the parking lot into your salon and lead clients into your services. Or, put photos of new styles on the floor and polyurethane over them; they will last for months. (Supermarkets are just beginning to sell floor space ads to their product manufacturers. Cruise a supermarket or two and see which ideas grab you.) It is hot; it is a new idea, and it works!

••

Summary

- Advertising agencies can help you promote your business by providing professional knowledge and experience.
- Print ads include newspaper and magazine ads.
- Radio and television ads are expensive, but can be beneficial in building your business.
- Net pages on the Internet are hot new ways to meet and greet customers.
- Coupons and mail offers give the client a reason to hold on to your ad and try your salon.
- All your advertisements should have one constant idea and create a household word of your salon's name!

Key Terms Defined

Circulation: The number of customers served by a particular medium—subscribers, listeners, or viewers reached.

Collateral: Any printed, promotional materials that your client can hold in her hand.

On-line Promotions: Putting coupons, sales information, and your address on a Web site on the Internet.

Penetrate the Market: Using several media, at once, to create a campaign that helps clients associate your name with hair services.

Point of Sale (POS): Any printed materials that help promote your business at the point where the customer makes a purchase.

planning a yearly calendar of advertising campaigns

IN THIS CHAPTER, YOU WILL LEARN:

- How to plan for *monthly promos*
- Easy ways to choose and use *seasonal promos*
- All about *holiday promos*
- How promotions help sell *retail items*
- The best use of promotions to reach *new residents*

KEY TERMS

- end caps
- loss leaders
- retail display
- speed bumps

MONTHLY PROMOTIONS

In Chapter 3, you learned that you must choose a business plan and keep records of your business. Once you have decided on your yearly budget for advertising and promotions, you should set up a calendar of promotions and ads that will stay within your budget and provide advertisement for those slow times of the year as well as bring new clients to your salon every month.

Look through the promotions in Chapter 10, or come up with ideas of your own and place them on your yearly calendar.

You may choose any assortment of promotions that fit your yearly budget, staff, and the type of clients that you are trying to reach. Once you decide on the promos you would like to use, meet with the staff and share your ideas. It is a good idea to clear the ideas with the staff and be sure there are no conflicts

YOUR CALENDAR OF MONTHLY PROMOS SHOULD LOOK SIMILAR TO THIS:

January: Super Bowl widow promo and perm ad (newspaper)

February: While you are here promo and face it promo

March: Easter bunny special promo and ad (radio)

April: The wet head is dead promo and fashion show

May: Prom promo and sisters save promo

June: June bride ad (newspaper) and single mingle promo

July: Dog days of summer promo, haircut promo, cut-a-thon promo, and take a moose to the beach promo

August: Color promo and retro hairstyle promo

September: Back to school cuts ad (radio) and nurses promo

October: Supervisors special, nail it promo, Internet promo

November: Wanted dead or alive promo, white gloves classes promo

December: Christmas and Hanukkah promos and New Year's resolution ad (runs simultaneously in newspaper and on radio)

or obvious mistakes. Remember, teamwork makes it more fun and a bigger success!

• •

Be sure to use your records and business plan from Chapter 3 as a guide to choosing your monthly promos.

• •

SEASONAL PROMOTIONS

There are promotions for every season of the year as well as the special events that take place in that season.

- Spring—New plants, new life, new attitudes, and new hairdo!
- Summer—Hot weather, beaches, vacation, and haircuts
- Fall—Back to school, leaves, and autumn haircolor changes
- Winter—Snowstorms, Christmas, Hanukkah and perm sales

Look through the promotions in Chapter 10 and find some seasonal promotions that can help you use the seasons of the year to build your business.

Certain yearly events in the community are great ideas for special promos.

- Every April and May plan a few perm and prom promos.
- June always suggests baseball and bridal promos.
- As football season starts, start Monday night haircut promos.

- As snow falls, think of ski, holiday, and gift certificate promos.

RETAIL PROMOS

Retail promos are probably the most fun to do! If you have imagination and creativity you can inspire many retail sales with retail promotions.

Just like a fine meal served in a luxurious restaurant, your presentation or **retail display** is everything. You could have the best selection of hair accessories, but if they are thrown in a box, they will not sell very well. Put those same hair accessories on a cute retail display and watch them sell like hotcakes!

Retail displays should always reflect which promotions you are doing. If you are in the middle of a perm sale, you should feature a display with perm care products. If you are having a color sale, set up a retail display for color-treated hair and sunscreen.

You will need to follow a few basic "Tricks of the Trade."

1. Clean it up! Be sure all retail displays stay fresh and clean; rotate old stock to the front and put new items in the back.

2. Take advantage of local events! Combine the local state fair concept with your display for retail by putting candy apples and state fair posters up or set up a display table with a football and college pennant on the day of the big game.

3. Create intrigue! Cover all mannequin eyes with sunglasses and set up a suntan product or eye makeup display!

4. Use one color! Stick to one color in a display—it is a real attention grabber.

5. Set up a clothesline and hang up retail bags, hair ornaments, and other retail items. Use pretty color cellophane wrap around each item. String the clothesline across the shampoo room, high above the sinks (gives the customer a view while you shampoo). Or, clip hair ornaments on the line and point a fan at them to create a breeze and lots of interest.

6. Buy a charcoal grill and set up a display in it for the summer. Make a sign that says, "Look what's cooking this week!" Change your items weekly and watch the sales sizzle.

7. Take a tip from the local supermarket—use end-of-the-aisle displays (called **end caps**) at the end of every station and shampoo bowl. Take a tour of the supermarket; they are retail experts, so borrow a few ideas from them.

8. Use **loss leaders!** A loss leader is an item that you sell at a phenomenally low price to get the customer over to your retail display, hoping she will buy other items. For example, set up a sale basket with all items $1 and put it next to the shampoo you really want to sell. While the customer is

looking through the sale basket, she may notice your real retail goal, shampoo.

9. Send your client back! Put the sale items in the back of the retail area or the back of the salon, so that the customer has to pass all the full-price items to get to the sale basket! It is not a coincidence that supermarkets walk you past full-price items to get to the sale racks in the back of the store; borrow the concept.

10. Dangerous duos! Ever go into the supermarket for chips and pick up dip, too? Notice where the dips are—right in front of the chips, right? You were inspired to buy the dip when you walked in to buy the chips. Do the same for your clients; put the retail items together in tempting displays that put duos together. (Put shampoo and conditioner together, hairpieces and wig cleaner together, etc.)

11. Create **speed bumps**. Do not leave the client a clean aisle out the door; set up a retail display that she has to go around. Note: Do not block fire exits and be sure the salon is accessible to the disabled.

12. Handwritten tags on a shelf create a greater awareness for the one or two items you would really like to sell. (Handwrite "Today only, 20% off" and hang the note from the shelf.)

13. Offer to honor drugstore shampoo coupons, up to $1 off, on your professional products.

Print a sign and put it in your window to announce it to the world.

14. Review floor advertising in Chapter 5. Use footsteps to lead clients to a particular display.

••

Take a tip from the window dresser and the department store merchandisers: Take a day trip and write down ideas, get inspired, and create your own retail wonderland!

••

Use window space to create interest in your salon. Inexpensive netting can create depth and color, just as retail can frame your photos—the possibilities are endless. You must have lots of creativity to be good at cosmetology, so put on your *creative cap* and go for it!

NEW-IN-TOWN PROMOS

The easiest to reach group of potential clients are the folks who are new in town. They have just relocated and are searching for a new stylist, so you can win them over easily! There are some easy ways to meet them.

1. Welcome Wagon: Almost every city has a "Welcome Wagon" type of program. These companies will bring a basket of samples and coupons to new residents in your community. Call them and ask to be included in the basket of samples. You can offer a bottle of shampoo or a brush with your name on it or a free first haircut

offer. You may even include your brochure.

2. New citizens clubs: Many clubs offer new neighbors companionship and fun activities. These clubs may be listed in the "What's Happening" section of your local newspaper. Call the clubs and offer to put on a hair demonstration or offer your salon as a meeting place for new members.

3. Human resource departments: Large companies have human resource departments that help relocate employees. Call them and offer a family discount to include in their benefit package.

4. Churches: Your local church will have a list of new members. Call and ask to send a congratulatory note and gift (shampoo or brush and a coupon).

5. Apartment complexes: Most apartment complexes have managers on the premises and keep a bulletin board and a newsletter. Contact them and offer to do a hair demonstration in their recreation room in exchange for a mention in the newsletter and on the bulletin board. Ask to have your business card included in the new resident information package.

6. Plan an open house every month, just for new neighbors. Put flyers up everywhere, put a press

release in the newspaper, and tell everyone you know.

Reaching new community members is easy. Think about where you would spend time if you were new in the area, then go there and walk around and talk to everyone you see! Perhaps you will start at the local zoo and end up at the laundromat, but smile, talk about hair, and distribute your business cards. You may also wish to send new residents a personal letter and introduce yourself and your salon.

TELEPHONE CARDS

A new type of advertising is really hot—a telephone card. It usually works like this:

1. you call the telephone company and tell them you are interested in the telephone card plan;

2. they print up cards for you to give out to clients when they spend money in your salon;

3. the client gets several minutes of free long-distance calls;

4. shop for the best prices—call all the long-distance carriers, especially the new ones, and get a real bargain;

5. advertising agencies can help you set up a telephone card offer; you can even have a key chain telephone card with your photo or logo on it.

Summary

- Plan a yearly calendar of promotions that offer something unique each month.
- Offer seasonal promotions.
- Plan holiday promotions far enough ahead to benefit from holiday shoppers.
- Be sure to plan retail promotions that change as inventory and seasonal changes occur.
- New neighbors make great customers—welcome them with open doors and coupons!
- Telephone cards are a great new way to offer a bonus to clients who use your services.

Key Terms Defined

End Caps: The display at the end of an aisle. This is the attention grabber at the front and the back of the aisle. In the salon, you could use the beginning and the end of the reception desk or shampoo bowls as an end cap.

Loss Leader: When you sell an item at a ridiculously low price to lure customers to what you really want them to buy. For example, you may offer hairspray at $1 per can and have your most profitable retail hairpieces in front of the hairspray.

Retail Display: The display set up to promote retail items. It may be pretty baskets full of items or shelves with eye-catching arrangements around them or even be a simple pyramid of bottles at the reception desk. Any time you arrange retail items to feature them, you have created a retail display.

Speed Bumps: Just like the speed bumps that slow you down in the parking lot, speed bumps in your salon should slow customers down so that they have to go around your retail display to get in and out of the salon.

calculating the cost for each promotion

IN THIS CHAPTER, YOU WILL LEARN:

- How to *appropriate* a portion of your yearly promotional budget for each promotion you plan
- What *co-op* dollars are and how to get them for your salon
- How to *calculate a discount* for each promotion
- Why you should *team up*
- How to *barter*

KEY TERMS

- barter
- break even point
- co-op advertising

IN CHAPTER 3, you learned that you need to prepare a yearly advertising/promotional budget. In Chapter 6, you learned that you must plan promotions for each month and season. Now you will learn that once you have set up your budget and your promotional plan, you must decide which portion of the monthly promotional budget you can afford to spend on each promotion (or ad) you wish to use for that month.

PERCENTAGE OF YEARLY BUDGET

In Chapter 10, we have included with every promotion a preparation page that will help you approximate the cost for that promotion. These preparation pages are essential because without a plan, you may overspend your entire yearly budget on one promotion. When you use a preparation sheet, you may decide that you might not get enough new clients from that particular promotion to justify the percentage of the yearly budget you would have to spend on that promotion. You may even decide that this is not the right promotion for you, and save your salon from wasting time, money, and energy on a promotion that may be ineffective. The preparation sheet for each promotion is as important as the promotion itself!

Once you have decided how much the promotion will cost, be sure you are not spending more than 20% of your yearly budget on any one promotion. Realize that you have to spread your promotion dollars throughout the entire year, so be careful and do not spend too much money on just one promotion! A great rule of thumb is to spend 4%–7% for most monthly promotions, and 8%–12% in months that are traditionally slow and need more promotions.

SAMPLE PROMOTIONAL BUDGET

January	.$600	July	.$400
February	.$200	August	.$400
March	.$200	September	.$450
April	.$350	October	.$550
May	.$250	November	.$600
June	.$400	December	.$600

Yearly Total: $5,000

Look at the pie chart below:

MONTHLY % SPENT ON PROMOTIONS

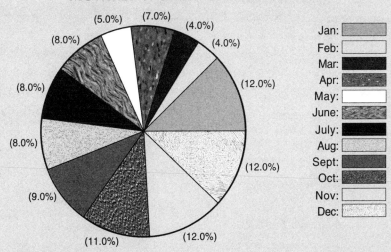

If the whole year's budget ($5,000) is the whole pie, each month is represented by a certain percentage and all the months add up to 100% of the pie ($5,000).

When you make a plan and stick to it, your promotional budget will always have enough capital to complete the year. If you overspend your budget, you may find yourself out of money in the months that you need it the most. *Stick to your budget!*

CO-OP ADVERTISING DOLLARS

In **co-op advertising**, certain manufacturers of products will give you money to help you advertise your salon if you mention their products in your ad. You and the manufacturer co-operatively contribute money to promote their products and your salon. The manufacturer may even give you the free ad slick for the newspaper or for making flyers, and give you additional dollars toward the ad, depending on how much money you spent with them in the past. (See Chapter 9 for more information on ad slicks.) For example, a manufacturer gave participating salons an ad slick (Figure 7–1) and co-op ad dollars to run it in the newspaper.

Co-op ads are a team effort which will be a winner for everyone involved!

- Your customer gets a discount!
- You get co-op ad dollars to promote your salon and help cut ad costs.
- The product manufacturer sells more product.

Call your product suppliers and ask them which manufacturers are offering co-op ad dollars and get involved in the co-op promotion!

CALCULATING THE DISCOUNT PERCENTAGE

Before you can offer a discount, you should be sure that you can afford it! Never offer a discount until you have figured out what your **break-even point** is.

Let's look at the cost of giving a perm and see how much profit we make on the perm and how much we can afford to discount it.

- Perm costs $8 each.
- Rods, endpapers, shampoo, conditioner, finish products cost about $2.
- Salon overhead should be considered (estimated at $25).
- Your pay needs to be considered (2 hours labor & benefits about $40).

The total estimated cost to give a perm is $75 each. This is your break-even point. You must charge at least $75 for the perm to be able to give the discount, yet stay in business.

Your salon charged $95 for each perm, so you can discount it $20 and still afford the sale. This discount is about 21% savings to the customer. You would want to round off the discount to an even 20% off sale!

Caution: Suppose the perm product cost you $28 each. Then you would not be able to afford the 20% discount.

FIGURE 7-1 Mousse ad slick used in co-op advertising

Use the following formula to figure out the cost.

1. List all the costs involved.
   - A perm costs $28 each
   - Rods, endpapers, shampoo, conditioner, finish products cost about $2
   - Salon overhead should be considered (estimated at $25)
   - Your pay needs to be considered (2 hours work and benefits about $40)

   Total the estimated cost to give perm = $95 each

2. Subtract the total estimated cost $95 from the price the salon charges for the perm $95

You can see that there is no room for a discount here; better try another perm on the worksheet and see if it is affordable.

1. List all the costs involved.
   - Perm costs $_____ each.
   - Rods, endpapers, shampoo, conditioner, finish products cost about $_____.
   - Salon overhead should be considered (estimated at $_____).
   - Your pay needs to be considered. (2 hours work and benefits about $_____).

   Total the estimated cost to give perm = $_____ each

2. Subtract the total estimated cost (break-even point) $_____ from the price the salon charges for the perm

3. List the difference here: _____.

Be sure to use a worksheet for every sale, discount, and promotion.

TEAMING UP WITH OTHER STORES

Most likely, many small stores in your neighborhood would love to team up with you and put on a promotion together with you.

Do a pedicure promotion with a local shoe store. Print up coupons good for a free pedicure with every purchase of sandals. Give the shoe store staff coupons to place in every box of sandals they sell this month. Have them place a poster in the entrance announcing the free offer. In exchange, you will place a poster in your lobby with a display of sandals from the store. Maybe you can pass out their flyers in your salon to every pedicure client.

Another idea for a team-up could be a local jeweler and wedding ring promotion for a free manicure.

Yet another idea for a great team-up is a fashion show with a local boutique. They do the clothes, you do the hair, and a local charity gets the profit. (Try PTAs—they love to do fashion shows.)

BARTERING

Barter means to trade or exchange. When you barter for services, you offer a haircut or a perm or some beauty service in exchange for helping you promote your business.

Usually, no money is involved, so you are able to put on a promotion with only a service given away.

You give free shampoo styles to all the clerks at the local movie theater for one week, and they wear a ribbon or a badge that says, "Ask me about my hair" or "Hairstyles by Gina Marie's Salon."

Try this barter offer with cosmetic clerks, bank tellers, nurses, dental hygienists, etc. The possibilities for these *barter buddies* are endless.

Calculating the cost for promotions and planning in advance can mean the difference in a successful promotional year or wasted advertising dollars. If you do not have a plan, you will never be able to reach your goal. If you do not have a goal, how will you ever be successful?

Make a plan and plan your work!

Summary

- You must calculate the cost of every promotion, before you decide to use it!
- Be sure to stick to your advertising budget for each promotion!
- Plan your discounts; be sure you can afford the discount and still break even!
- Team up with other local small businesses and promote each other!
- Barter your way through promotions; it doesn't cost a thing!

Key Terms Defined

Barter: Trading or exchanging your services for a free mention of your name and salon services. Bartering means that you do not pay someone (with money) to promote you; instead you pay each other by exchanging services.

Break-Even Point: The amount of money you must charge for a service and still break even on the discount. Never discount any service for more money than the service costs you to perform. Always be sure you will at least break even after the promotion is over.

Co-op Advertising: Teaming up with a product manufacturer that helps you promote your services if you include its product in your promotion. The manufacturer gives you money to help defray the cost of the ad. In exchange for the co-op money, you mention the manufacturer in your ad.

are you sure you want to offer a sale?

IN THIS CHAPTER, YOU WILL LEARN:

- How to hold a sale and still make money on the service
- When a sale can hurt you more than help you
- Why some salons end up with *sale only* clients
- How to hold *usual* sales
- What a *one day sale* is

KEY TERMS

- one day sale
- sale only clients
- selected stylists

IN THIS CHAPTER, you will learn to decide whether or not you should offer a sale to your clients. Sometimes, a sale can be the perfect vehicle to create new interest in a service or to bring in new clients. Other times, however, a sale can hurt the salon more than it helps. In Chapter 7 you learned that you must figure the cost of the service before you can offer a discount. You must always be able to break even when you offer a service. If you offer many sales and you lose money on services often enough, you will put yourself out of business.

Before you even consider a sale as a means to promotion, you should exhaust all of your other options. Chapter 10 has many ideas that do not discount your prices. Actually, if you use a little creative genius, you can think of promotions that would bring you plenty of new clients and not force you to discount your prices. But, at times, the only suitable promotion is a sale.

Tips for Sales

- Be sure your sale does not discount your prices so much that you have less cash than before the sale.

- Use the formula and worksheets in Chapter 7 and be sure you will at least break even.

- Plan the sale for a time when salons are traditionally slow (January, July, and after long weekends).

- Never offer a sale for a month before a national holiday or during the back-to-school rush.

- Never put your best-selling perm or color service on sale; discount one that you would like to introduce or to increase sales.

- Try to re-book every sale client for another service (cut, color, nails, etc.). Try to make the sale client a regular one.

- If, during the planning stages, you find that the sale will be too costly, toss out the sale idea and try another promotion.

SALE-ONLY CLIENTELE

There are customers who only have a perm when a perm sale is on. Some salons have traditional perm sales, at the same date, every year! For example, one department store has a perm sale every 4 months. Another salon chain runs a sale twice a year.

Try to offer only one traditional sale per year and schedule the other sales in a slow month when you have nothing to lose. Stagger them to different times, so that new clients can take advantage of the sales, but **"sale-only clients"** cannot plan on them.

Many customers wait for the sales to have their perms at a discount price. They are **"sale-only clients"** and you will never see them come in for a perm unless you have a sale. You probably cannot encourage them to become regular clients or to try other services. Some of these clients have limited income and must rely on a sale to afford the service. They traditionally do not buy retail products for home use and they are only loyal customers until the salon down the street offers the same perm at a lower price. You cannot build your business on these clients. Use them as a filler to boost up your appointment books during slow months!

Use sales only as a last resort, not every month!

SELECTED STYLISTS ONLY

If you are already fully booked with clients and you offer a sale for the entire salon, rather than for selected stylists, you are discounting work that you would have done anyway, so you have lost money.

A stylist who is already busy does not need to participate in sales.

A great way to offer a sale for new stylists and not cause busier stylists to lose money is to be sure to state the following in every ad or promotion that you do:

- this offer is good only with participating stylists;

or

- sale applies only to services booked with Gina and Joe;

or

- sale price offered by selected stylists, only.

This allows new stylists to build a business and does not hurt a more seasoned stylist's sales.

ONE DAY SALES

This is probably the best invention since sliced bread! If you prepare for the sale, budget your profits, and plan ahead, you could be booked for a year with the response from this sale.

One day sales work like this:

1. you place an ad in the newspaper, announcing the one day sale of certificates;

2. you will be very busy that day; be sure you have extra help at the desk, to answer the telephone and sell certificates over the telephone, while you handle the crowd in the salon;

3. perform no services that day; simply sell the certificates and take the money on that day;

4. make appointments for people who want to redeem their coupons right away;

5. open a special savings account to deposit the money into, so that as a coupon is redeemed during the next year you can withdraw that amount and pay your register for the coupon;

6. stock up on the perm that you offered. Be sure you have a sufficient amount of that brand;

7. have extra credit card receipts and sales checks ready;

8. purchase gift certificates to give the client when she pays for the half-price perm. Be sure to attach a copy of the ad and flyer, so that she will understand that the certificate is good:

   With selected stylists

   On the advertised brand only

   To be used on Monday, Tuesday, and Wednesday only in 1997

   You may even wish to put the above three rules on every certificate you sell;

9. use a newspaper ad, flyers, and handouts to announce the one day sale; (See Chapter 5 to refresh yourself on ads and Chapter 9 will help you use flyers.)

10. *have fun with the one day sale.* Bake goodies and serve coffee that day. Use doilies on the trays of cookies and real china coffee cups (rented, of course);

ONE DAY PERM SALE

Gina's Salon

Is Proud to Offer You

Our $100 Perm for *Only $50*

Glorious curls, perms at half-price

•

Stop in or call on Monday, June 15, to purchase a certificate for a perm, which can be used any Monday, Tuesday or Wednesday in 1997, with selected stylists.

•

Certificates must be purchased on July 15 to receive the half-price offer. All certificates must be paid in full on the 15th of June.

•

Cash, checks, credit cards accepted. Phone orders taken with credit cards.

•

Offer limited to three coupons per client.

Phone: 332•3425 • Fax: 665•1214

$100 Perm Certificate $100 Perm Certificate

SALON NAME

Authorized Signature

Expiration Date

Valid

$100 Perm Certificate $100 Perm Certificate

FIGURE 8-1 Promotion for a one day sale

11. document all transactions and number all certificates. Record all sales, especially cash sales. If your client lost the certificate, you may want to look up the record and void it out;

12. be sure to personally sign all certificates to avoid copies and fraud.

Summary

- Sales can be a great way to meet and court new clients.
- Be sure to offer sales only after all other avenues of promotion have been tried.
- Sales should be planned and you should always break even (at least) on a sale.
- Salons that offer too many sales end up with a sale only clientele that never purchases services at full price.
- Most sales should be offered with selected stylists only.
- One day sales can book you for the year—be sure to follow the guidelines and prepare for the deluge of one day sale clients.
- Keep good records and keep sale certificates under lock and key—they represent cash.

Key Terms Defined

One Day Sale: Certificates for perms that are sold on only one day per year, yet are redeemable for an entire year. They are usually sold at half-price and redeemed with selected stylists only.

Sale Only Clients: Clients who come to you only when you are offering a sale. They never purchase services at full price; they wait for a sale.

Selected Stylists: New or not-so-busy stylists who usually participate in sales. Older, more established stylists do not need to offer sales to keep booked; they would lose money if they participated in the sales.

flyers, flyers, flyers

IN THIS CHAPTER, YOU WILL LEARN:

- How to *develop a flyer*
- That flyers give you a *big return* at a modest cost
- How to use *ad slicks* and *velox*
- The *purpose of using computer graphics* to create flyers
- How to time the *use of flyers* to tie into local events
- Where to use flyers
- Where you may not distribute flyers

KEY TERMS

- ad slicks
- computer graphics
- software
- velox

DEVELOPING FLYERS

Flyers are easy to develop or create. Anything you see in print can be made into a flyer. You can use colored paper, different shapes and sizes, and different themes. Many promotions in Chapter 10 can be made into flyers.

Flyers should have a few main ingredients:

1. be clear and uncluttered. Do not put too much into the flyer; if it is too busy, it will not be read;

2. give the client a reason to keep the flyer: put a coupon on it;

3. your salon name and telephone number must always be included in the flyer;

4. your promotion or sale should be clearly outlined;

5. a picture is worth more than a thousand words; use pictures, photos, and graphics in the flyer;

6. print ads make great flyers, too!

Printing companies can set up flyers for you or you can draw your own if you are artistic or creative.

LOW COST AND HIGH RETURN

Probably no other promotion will bring you the same amount of results with such little financial investment. Flyers cost fractions of a cent and can be used to:

- stuff bags
- post on bulletin boards
- mail out to clients
- exchange with neighboring businesses
- hand out at special events

Once you have used a flyer, set up a file and keep it for future use. Sometimes only the date will change and you will have an instant flyer at your fingertips.

VELOX AND AD SLICKS

When you purchase and place an ad in any newspaper or magazine, insist that they provide you with a copy of the ad that is on smooth paper and makes clear copies of the ad. This smooth copy of the ad is called a **velox** or an **ad slick**.

••••••••••••••••••••••••••••••••

When you place an ad, *always* remember to ask for the ad slick. You paid the production costs when you paid for the ad!

••••••••••••••••••••••••••••••••

Use the ad slick in any copier and you have professional flyers with the touch of a button!

COMPUTER GRAPHICS

Almost everyone has a personal computer (PC) in the home or office or is able to rent one. Many inexpensive programs and **software** packages are available that will enable you to create flyers by copying the **computer graphics** (pictures on the computer software program) to a text that you typed in a word processing program. Graphics help to make the ad come alive!

••••••••••••••••••••••••••••••••

Classes offered at computer stores and community colleges will help you learn to use a PC and software packages. There may even be a college or high school student who is willing to help you in exchange for a haircut. Call the computer science department of your local schools for more information.

••••••••••••••••••••••••••••••••

DISTRIBUTING FLYERS

Timing

You can get the most out of your flyers if you tie them into a local or national event or holiday.

For example, use a flyer with a sports theme during the Olympics. Use a ladies discount flyer the week of Mother's Day, or offer a nurses discount on the day the local college opens a nursing program. Tie in with local heroes: if your local school won a homecoming game, use the idea and do a flyer to pass out at the parade to celebrate the win; if the city tennis league wins the national competition, create a tennis sale flyer.

Use all holidays—always have a flyer ready for the upcoming holiday. If there is a reason to celebrate or a special occasion coming up, you should have a flyer to accompany it. Tie in with all civic events and pass out flyers on the big day.

Location

Certain locations are perfect for flyer distribution.

- Bulletin boards, meetings, civic events, and neighborhoods.

- Never leave the supermarket without putting some of your latest flyers on the community bulletin boards.

- Local businesses have bulletin boards at time clocks and lunchrooms; ask their human resources department if you can post flyers on them.

- Hospitals and colleges as well as local day care centers and schools may have bulletin boards to post flyers on; call ahead and get permission first.

- Do not forget apartment complexes and laundromats—they always have bulletin boards.

- Health spas are great places to distribute flyers, too.

Keep some flyers in your car and always keep one or two in your purse. You never know where you will find a place to post one!

There are several places that you should *never* stick flyers.

1. Mailboxes—unless you use the U.S. Postal Service, and actually purchase postage, you are defrauding the government by putting a flyer in or on a mailbox. *Never put a flyer in a mailbox.*

2. On windshields. Nothing upsets a shopping center or apartment complex owner more than a few hundred of your flyers to clean up. People toss them on the ground or they blow away and you make more enemies than clients!

3. Do not stick flyers to houses, doors, or cars by using cellophane adhesive tape. When the client pulls off the flyer, paint comes off with it and you have lost a potential client and made an enemy.

4. Do not pass out flyers in a mall or a shopping center without getting permission, in writing, at the mall office. If you are caught passing out flyers on private property, without permission, you could be arrested and charged with soliciting or trespassing. Remember, the businesses in that mall pay a high rent and it includes the privilege to exclusive rights to promote themselves in that mall. They may not want you there, so always get permission first.

Summary

▷ Flyers are a great way to promote your business for a very small cash investment.

▷ You can develop flyers from any printed material.

▷ Use ad slicks or velox copies of your ads—create your own flyers.

▷ Use computer graphics to make inexpensive yet effective flyers.

▷ Tie flyers into current events.

▷ Use bulletin boards to display your flyers.

▷ Get permission before posting flyers.

▷ Never stick flyers on cars or in mailboxes.

▷ Never distribute flyers at a mall, unless you have written permission.

Key Terms Defined

Ad Slicks: The shiny copy of your printed ad, which can be used to make instant flyers.

Computer Graphics: The artwork that you take off a software program on your PC and use to create a flyer.

Software: Programs installed on a computer that allow specific functions with that computer. Some software packages are spreadsheets, some are data bases, some are word processing programs, and some are graphic design programs.

Velox: Another term for ad slick. This is not used much anymore, but you may hear someone call an ad slick by this name.

promotions

Here are some promotions that you can use to create your own ideas for a successful salon promo! Utilize the wording and images to develop an advertisement or flyer to fit your salon.

INDEX

1. Take a Mousse to the Beach. . . . 69
2. Kid's Cuts Tee-Shirts 72
3. Supervisor's Special. 75
4. Bad Weather Promo. 78
5. Internet Promo 81
6. Men Only Night 84
7. New Customers Cuts Specials . . 87
8. Nurses Promo. 90
9. Nail It! 93
10. Face It! 96
11. Professional Courtesy Hours . . . 99
12. Mother's Day Special 102
13. Father's Day Special 105
14. Easter Bunny Special 108
15. Christmas Stocking Stuffers. . . . 111
16. Holiday Glitz and Glamour. 114
17. Vacation Extravaganza 117
18. The Wet Head is Dead 120
19. Sports Fans Promo. 123
20. 2 Fers 126
21. Sisters Save 129
22. Cut-a-Thon 132
23. Buttons, Buttons, Buttons 135
24. Back to School Stickers 138
25. For the New Neighbors 141
26. An Island Escape 144
27. Singles Mingle 147
28. The Finish Is on Us! 150
29. Dog Days of Summer 153
30. Try It On. 156
31. Superbowl Widow's
    Special 159
32. Upside Down Ad
    (Local Paper) 162
33. Forgive Us for Not Contacting
    You Sooner! 165
34. A Cut for the Young Master! . . . 168
35. Little Girl's Birthday Party 171
36. You Pick the Discount 174
37. We Need Models. 177
38. 100,000 Mile Overhaul 180
39. A Sweetheart of a Sale. 183
40. Champions Promo 186
41. Hot Haircuts—Cool Prices. 189
42. Name Our New Style Contest. . 192
43. Retro Hairstyle Photo Contest . 195
44. Private Issue 198
45. How to Get Your Man Promo . . 201

46. First Haircut for $1 204
47. Spring/Watch It Grow 207
48. Family Special 210
49. Color You Changed 213
50. Mail to Males 216
51. Birthday Card Coupon 219
52. Guess What's Missing 222
53. One Day Perm Sale 225
54. Cut Cards 228
55. Customer Appreciation Days . . 231
56. Promo Cards for the Mirrors . . 234
57. Here Comes the Bride 237
58. Wanted Dead or Alive 240
59. Salute to Paris 243
60. An Investment in Your
    Appearance 246
61. Afternoon Delight 249
62. Shoe Biz Promo 252
63. Have Lunch at Our Place 255
64. Temps Deserve a Break 258
65. Beat the Blues 261
66. Book Worm Promo 264
67. College Dorm—Sorority
    Promotion 267
68. What's Hot and What's Not 270
69. Seniors Seminars 273
70. Granddaughter's First
    Manicure 276
71. Community Theater 279
72. Anchor Team Makeovers 282
73. Health Hair Promo 285
74. Father and Son Haircut Day . . . 288
75. Members Only 291
76. "The Worst Thing I Ever Did
    to My Hair" Contest 294
77. Jazzy Specials for When You
    Have the Blues 297
78. New Mom Makeovers 300
79. White Gloves Classes for
    Young Ladies 303

80. Kid's Coloring Contest 306
81. Beehive Contest 309
82. New Career Makeovers 312
83. A Day of Beauty Gift
    Certificate 315
84. Red, White and Blue Sale 318
85. Cowgirls—Two Step Promo 321
86. May Day Makeovers 324
87. Form Determines Function
    Promo 327
88. Nineteenth Hole Pedicure 330
89. Nail Art Promo 333
90. Wrap It Up 336
91. Teacher's Pet 339
92. Swimmers Specials 342
93. Ski Club Promo 345
94. Salesclerk Promo 348
95. Makeover Party for the
    Wedding Party 351
96. Book a Year's Cuts and Save . . . 354
97. It Is In The Bag 357
98. Manage That Mane 360
99. First Day of School, Cuts
    on the House! 363
100. Frequent Haircut Card 366
101. Fix It Day Promo 369
102. Wig Care Week 372
103. Prom Day Promo 375
104. Photo Finish (Glamour
     Makeovers) 378
105. Dieter's Reward Promo 381
106. Engagement Ring Promo 384
107. Garden Club Promo 387
108. Realtors Promo 390
109. Choir Members Special
     Promo 393
110. Smooth Sailing Beach
     Haircuts 396
111. Cruise in Promo 399

TAKE A MOUSSE
TO
THE BEACH
FREE!

With every perm this month
receive a
FREE MOUSSE...
with sunscreen

Salon Name
Address
Phone

TAKE A MOUSSE TO THE BEACH PROMOTION

Objective
✄Reach new perm and retail clients. Help perms last longer at the beach! Reduce perm redos from abuse.

Description
✄Offer a free can of mousse with sunscreen in it, for all customers who purchase a perm this summer.

Preparation
✄**Two Months Before:** Place an ad in newspaper and get copy of the ad slick to use for flyers. (Buy neon paper to run flyers on.)

Stock several cases of mousse. Check for co-op money with mousse manufacturers. The company that made the mousse may offer rebates to help you with the promo cost.

✄**One Month Before:** Distribute flyers as bag stuffers (swimsuit stores, resorts, beach hotels, schools).

Notify current clients by posting a flyer on your bulletin board for a month previous to the promotion.

Meet with salon staff and explain the promo to everyone. Give all a stack of flyers to distribute.

✄**One Week Before:** Double check with the newspaper, be sure you have enough mousse; display it in salon.

✄**One Day Before the Ad Runs:** Review promo with staff. Make copy of the tracking sheet.

Estimated Cost
✄$20-30 if only flyers used. Additional cost for newspaper ad—depends on ad size and newspaper rates. Also, remember to allocate additional retail $ for extra mousse needed. After the promotion—redistribute retail dollars for other products.

PROMOTION TRACKING SHEET

(Keep This on a Clipboard at the Reception Desk)

_____

NAME OF PROMOTION

_____ _____

DATE PROMO STARTS   DATE PROMO ENDS

_____

AMOUNT OF NEW CUSTOMERS

	SUN	MON	TUE	WED	THU	FRI	SAT
Week 1							
Week 2							
Week 3							
Week 4							
Monthly Total							

(At the end of every day, take a moment to jot down the number of clients this promotion brought in. At the end of the promotion, total all of the weekly results for a grand total of client responses to this promotion. Be sure to note bad weather, illness, or any mishaps that may have interfered with your promotion's potential success.)

FREE

KID'S
TEE-SHIRT
THIS WEEK
ONLY

FREE TEE-SHIRTS
FOR EVERY CHILD WHO
HAS A HAIRCUT IN
OUR SALON

SALON NAME
ADDRESS
PHONE

Offer Limited To Children Under 12

KID'S TEE-SHIRT PROMOTION

Objective
✄ Reach new children and families as clients.

Description
✄ Offer a free tee-shirt with every haircut purchased.

Preparation
✄ **Two Months Before:** Place an ad in newspaper or make flyers. Get a copy of the ad slick and copy flyers on neon colored paper.

Make tee-shirts by purchasing plain tee-shirts and stenciling the salon name on them, or have a tee-shirt made that says: "I love my haircut from XYZ's salon." Make the shirt look like a child wrote it, use backward letters and a child's hand print on it. Let a child design it! (A design-a-shirt promo?)

✄ **One Month Before:** Distribute flyers as bag stuffers (nursery schools, kids clubs, etc.). Notify current clients by posting a flyer on your bulletin board for a month previous to the promotion.

Meet with salon staff and explain the promo to everyone. Give all a stack of flyers to distribute.

✄ **One Week Before:** Double check with the newspaper, be sure you have enough tee-shirts—display them in the salon window.

✄ **One Day Before the Ad Runs:** Review promo with staff. Make copy of the tracking sheet.

Estimated Cost
✄ **Printing costs:** $20–30 if only flyers used. Additional cost for—depends on ad size and newspaper rates. Tee-shirt costs vary—get several estimates before purchasing. (Any shirts left over make great giveaways for contests.)

PROMOTION TRACKING SHEET

(Keep This on a Clipboard at the Reception Desk)

_____

NAME OF PROMOTION

_____   _____

DATE PROMO STARTS   DATE PROMO ENDS

_____

AMOUNT OF NEW CUSTOMERS

	SUN	MON	TUE	WED	THU	FRI	SAT
Week 1							
Week 2							
Week 3							
Week 4							
Monthly Total							

(At the end of every day, take a moment to jot down the number of clients this promotion brought in. At the end of the promotion, total all of the weekly results for a grand total of client responses to this promotion. Be sure to note bad weather, illness, or any mishaps that may have interfered with your promotion's potential success.)

ATTN:

SHIFT WORKERS
SUPERVISOR'S SPECIAL
(While Our Supervisor Sleeps)

RECEIVE
ALL LATE NIGHT SERVICES
PERFORMED

11 PM – 3 AM

AT

HALF-PRICE!

SALON NAME
ADDRESS
PHONE NUMBER

SUPERVISOR'S SPECIAL—SHIFT WORKERS
HALF-PRICE SERVICES PROMOTION

Objective
✀ Gain new clients for late night appointments.

Description
✀ Any services given in the appointed time are half-price.

Preparation
✀ **One Month Before:** Make and distribute flyers.

Notify current clients by posting a flyer on your bulletin board for a month previous to the promotion.

Meet with salon staff and explain the promo to everyone. Give all a stack of flyers to distribute.

Estimated Cost
✀ $20-30 if only flyers used. Be sure you can afford the sale—use chapters 7 and 8 to figure the cost of the discount.

PROMOTION TRACKING SHEET

(Keep This on a Clipboard at the Reception Desk)

_____

NAME OF PROMOTION

_____   _____

DATE PROMO STARTS   DATE PROMO ENDS

_____

AMOUNT OF NEW CUSTOMERS

	SUN	MON	TUE	WED	THU	FRI	SAT
Week 1							
Week 2							
Week 3							
Week 4							
Monthly Total							

(At the end of every day, take a moment to jot down the number of clients this promotion brought in. At the end of the promotion, total all of the weekly results for a grand total of client responses to this promotion. Be sure to note bad weather, illness, or any mishaps that may have interfered with your promotion's potential success.)

WHILE YOU ARE HERE–
Bad Weather Promotion

Print up copies of a note pad
similar to this one

To _____ *Our Clients* _____

WHILE YOU ARE HERE TODAY

_____ *Ms. Judy Ventura,* _____

Beauty Salon Supervisor

_____

TELEPHONED		PLEASE CALL	
CALLED TO SEE YOU		WILL CALL AGAIN	
WANTS TO SEE YOU		URGENT	
WANTS TO OFFER YOU A DISCOUNT		☑	

Message _____ *Save 50%* _____

on an additional

service while you

are in the salon today

_____
Operator

PUT THEM AT EVERY STATION
AND THE FRONT DESK

Every time it snows or the weather causes clients to
cancel appointments, whip out the pad and offer
every client **currently in the salon**, a chance to have
a half-price service with the **purchase of the
services she is currently having**.

• • •

Because you have cancellations, you will
have time to try new colors or styles!

WHILE YOU ARE HERE—BAD WEATHER PROMOTION

Objective
✂ Generate additional sales on slow days.

Description
✂ Hand out the discount slips to clients in the salon.

Preparation
✂ Meet with salon staff and explain the promo to everyone. Give all a pad to tuck away for a rainy day!

Estimated Cost
✂ $20–50 printing costs

PROMOTION TRACKING SHEET

(Keep This on a Clipboard at the Reception Desk)

_____
NAME OF PROMOTION

_____   _____
DATE PROMO STARTS   DATE PROMO ENDS

_____
AMOUNT OF NEW CUSTOMERS

	SUN	MON	TUE	WED	THU	FRI	SAT
Week 1							
Week 2							
Week 3							
Week 4							
Monthly Total							

(At the end of every day, take a moment to jot down the number of clients this promotion brought in. At the end of the promotion, total all of the weekly results for a grand total of client responses to this promotion. Be sure to note bad weather, illness, or any mishaps that may have interfered with your promotion's potential success.)

ATTN: INTERNET USERS:

**Pulling your hair out
while you struggle to
find a certain web page?**

YOU JUST FOUND A WINNER!

Print this page out and bring it in
when you have your next haircut...
and will give you a free mouse pad.

A FREE MOUSE PAD

SALON NAME

**ADDRESS
INTERNET ADDRESS
PHONE NUMBER**

INTERNET PROMOTION

Objective

✂ Reach new haircut clients through the internet.

Description

✂ Set up a web page on the internet. Offer the free mouse pad with a haircut.

Preparation

✂ **One Month Before:** Buy pads at local computer store. Stencil your salon logo on them (or if price allows, order them custom made).

Notify current clients by posting a flyer on your bulletin board for a month previous to the promotion. (Just print out the web page and duplicate it.)

Meet with salon staff and explain the promo to everyone. Give all a mouse pad to display!

✂ **One Day Before the Web Site Begins:** Review promo with staff and make copy of the tracking sheet.

Estimated Cost

✂ $20–100 for mouse pads, depending on artwork. $100–1,000 for a website. Get estimates first. You may be able to afford a bulletin board if a website is too costly.

PROMOTION TRACKING SHEET

(Keep This on a Clipboard at the Reception Desk)

_____

NAME OF PROMOTION

_____   _____

DATE PROMO STARTS   DATE PROMO ENDS

_____

AMOUNT OF NEW CUSTOMERS

	SUN	MON	TUE	WED	THU	FRI	SAT
Week 1							
Week 2							
Week 3							
Week 4							
Monthly Total							

(At the end of every day, take a moment to jot down the number of clients this promotion brought in. At the end of the promotion, total all of the weekly results for a grand total of client responses to this promotion. Be sure to note bad weather, illness, or any mishaps that may have interfered with your promotion's potential success.)

MEN ONLY NIGHT!

EVERY MONDAY NIGHT OUR SALON CLOSES IT'S DOORS TO ALL WOMEN!

✄

MONDAY NIGHT FOOTBALL BOOMS FROM 4 TV SETS, MEN'S SERVICES ARE DISCOUNTED 10% AND SNACKS ARE ON THE HOUSE!

✄

JOIN YOUR BUDDIES!

✄

IT'S A MAN THING!!

✄

BOOK YOUR APPOINTMENT NOW!

SALON NAME
ADDRESS
PHONE

MEN ONLY PROMOTION

Objective
✄ Reach more male clients.

Description
✄ Close the salon to women, plug in 4 TVs and let the men watch the big game, snack, visit together, and have services in your salon.

Preparation
✄ **Two Months Before**: Make and distribute flyers. Contact newspaper if you are using an ad.

✄ **One Month Before**: Notify current clients by posting a flyer on your bulletin board for a month previous to the promotion.

Meet with salon staff and explain the promo to everyone. Give all a stack of flyers to distribute.

✄ **One Week Before**: Double check with the newspaper, get a copy of the ad slick and run off your flyers on neon colored paper. Be sure you have enough snacks and TVs on hand!

✄ **One Day Before The Ad Runs**: Review promo with staff. Make copy of the tracking sheet. Secure TVs.

Estimated Cost
✄ $20–30 if only flyers used. Additional cost for newspaper ad—depends on ad size and newspaper rates. Also, remember snacks cost a few dollars, and must be fresh. Ask each stylist to bring in a TV.

PROMOTION TRACKING SHEET

(Keep This on a Clipboard at the Reception Desk)

_____
NAME OF PROMOTION

_____   _____
DATE PROMO STARTS   DATE PROMO ENDS

_____
AMOUNT OF NEW CUSTOMERS

	SUN	MON	TUE	WED	THU	FRI	SAT
Week 1							
Week 2							
Week 3							
Week 4							
Monthly Total							

(At the end of every day, take a moment to jot down the number of clients this promotion brought in. At the end of the promotion, total all of the weekly results for a grand total of client responses to this promotion. Be sure to note bad weather, illness, or any mishaps that may have interfered with your promotion's potential success.)

A Reason to try Us

PLACE YOUR STAFF PHOTO HERE

SALON NAME
ADDRESS
PHONE

WE TREAT OUR CUSTOMERS TO A FREE HAIRCUT
WITH THE PURCHASE OF ANY OTHER SERVICE.

Call for an appointment

NEW CLIENT HAIRCUT PROMOTION

Objective

✄ Reach new clients as they move into town.

Description

✄ Flyers distributed to welcome wagon, human resources departments of local companies, etc.

Preparation

✄ **One Month Before:** Distribute flyers. Meet with salon staff and explain the promo to everyone. Give all a stack of flyers to distribute. Make copy of the tracking sheet.

Estimated Cost

✄ $20-30 if only flyers used.

PROMOTION TRACKING SHEET

(Keep This on a Clipboard at the Reception Desk)

_____
NAME OF PROMOTION

_____   _____
DATE PROMO STARTS   DATE PROMO ENDS

_____
AMOUNT OF NEW CUSTOMERS

	SUN	MON	TUE	WED	THU	FRI	SAT
Week 1							
Week 2							
Week 3							
Week 4							
Monthly Total							

(At the end of every day, take a moment to jot down the number of clients this promotion brought in. At the end of the promotion, total all of the weekly results for a grand total of client responses to this promotion. Be sure to note bad weather, illness, or any mishaps that may have interfered with your promotion's potential success.)

Nurses Deserve a Break

SALON NAME

is pleased to offer

A SALE FOR NURSES ONLY

Wear your uniform when you have an appointment and

Receive a 20% Discount

PHONE NUMBER

Address

Offer limited to July & August 1997 only

NURSES DISCOUNT PROMOTION

Objective
✂ Reach new clients by offering nurses a discount.

Description
✂ Flyers mailed to every hospital and doctors office in town.

Preparation
✂ **One Month Before:** Distribute flyers.

Notify current clients by posting a flyer on your bulletin board for a month previous to the promotion.

Meet with salon staff and explain the promo to everyone. Give all a stack of flyers to distribute.

✂ **One Day Before:** Review promo with staff. Make copy of the tracking sheet.

Estimated Cost
✂ $20-30 if only flyers used.

PROMOTION TRACKING SHEET

(Keep This on a Clipboard at the Reception Desk)

_____

NAME OF PROMOTION

_____   _____

DATE PROMO STARTS   DATE PROMO ENDS

_____

AMOUNT OF NEW CUSTOMERS

	SUN	MON	TUE	WED	THU	FRI	SAT
Week 1							
Week 2							
Week 3							
Week 4							
Monthly Total							

(At the end of every day, take a moment to jot down the number of clients this promotion brought in. At the end of the promotion, total all of the weekly results for a grand total of client responses to this promotion. Be sure to note bad weather, illness, or any mishaps that may have interfered with your promotion's potential success.)

Nail It!

**TRY
ONE
<u>FREE</u>
ACRYLIC
NAIL**

Today, while you are visiting our salon.

**This is a chance for you to try the nails
you have always dreamed of.**

NAIL IT PROMOTION

Objective
✂ Let clients try a free acrylic nail that they may have been afraid to try.

Description
✂ Give any current client a chance to try this additional service. This is a great promo for a slow day, or a super way to introduce a new nail technician to clients.

Preparation
✂ **One Day Before:** Notify current clients by posting a flyer on your bulletin board.

Meet with salon staff and explain the promo to everyone. Give all a stack of lyers to distribute.

Stock up on nail products.

Estimated Cost
✂ $20 for flyers

PROMOTION TRACKING SHEET

(Keep This on a Clipboard at the Reception Desk)

_____

NAME OF PROMOTION

_____   _____

DATE PROMO STARTS   DATE PROMO ENDS

_____

AMOUNT OF NEW CUSTOMERS

	SUN	MON	TUE	WED	THU	FRI	SAT
Week 1							
Week 2							
Week 3							
Week 4							
Monthly Total							

(At the end of every day, take a moment to jot down the number of clients this promotion brought in. At the end of the promotion, total all of the weekly results for a grand total of client responses to this promotion. Be sure to note bad weather, illness, or any mishaps that may have interfered with your promotion's potential success.)

Face It!

Today, while you are visiting our salon...

Try a
FREE
15 Minute
Facial

This is a chance for you to try the facial you have always deserved and never tried!

SALON NAME
NUMBER

Put your face in our hands.

FACE IT PROMOTION

Objective

✂ Let clients try a 15 minute mini facial, free. You can acquaint clients with facial services they may have been afraid to try.

Description

✂ Give any current client a chance to try this additional service. This is a great promo for a slow day, or a super way to introduce a new skin technician to clients.

Preparation

✂ **One Day Before:** Notify current clients by posting a flyer on your bulletin board. Meet with salon staff and explain the promo to everyone. Give all a stack of flyers to distribute.

Stock up on facial products and be sure the facial room is sparkling clean!

Estimated Cost

✂ $20 for flyers

PROMOTION TRACKING SHEET

(Keep This on a Clipboard at the Reception Desk)

_____

NAME OF PROMOTION

_____   _____

DATE PROMO STARTS   DATE PROMO ENDS

_____

AMOUNT OF NEW CUSTOMERS

	SUN	MON	TUE	WED	THU	FRI	SAT
Week 1							
Week 2							
Week 3							
Week 4							
Monthly Total							

(At the end of every day, take a moment to jot down the number of clients this promotion brought in. At the end of the promotion, total all of the weekly results for a grand total of client responses to this promotion. Be sure to note bad weather, illness, or any mishaps that may have interfered with your promotion's potential success.)

Professional Courtesy Appointments

Our Salon is pleased to announce:

A special, professional courtesy appointment for you!

We will open an hour earlier, exclusively for your convenience.

BEFORE YOU GO TO WORK AT
YOUR COSMETIC COUNTER, STOP IN FOR A
QUICK MANICURE, BLOW DRY, OR SET. WE WILL GET
YOU READY FOR THE DAY AND GET YOU OUT THE
DOOR ON TIME, **WE GUARANTEE IT!**

Salon Name
Address
Phone

PROFESSIONAL COURTESY PROMOTION

Objective

✄ Invite cosmetic salespersons, technicians from nail service only salons, and sales professionals in the beauty field, to come in for a quick fix on the way to work.

Description

✄ Open one hour earlier and give these clients first option at these appointments.

Preparation

✄ *One Month Before*: Make and distribute flyers to the professionals you are inviting.

Notify current clients by posting a flyer on your bulletin board for a month previous to the promotion.

Meet with salon staff and explain the promo to everyone. Give all a stack of flyers to distribute. Secure extra staff as needed.

Estimated Cost

✄ $20 if only flyers used.

PROMOTION
TRACKING SHEET

(Keep This on a Clipboard at the Reception Desk)

_____

NAME OF PROMOTION

_____   _____

DATE PROMO STARTS   DATE PROMO ENDS

_____

AMOUNT OF NEW CUSTOMERS

	SUN	MON	TUE	WED	THU	FRI	SAT
Week 1							
Week 2							
Week 3							
Week 4							
Monthly Total							

(At the end of every day, take a moment to jot down the number of clients this promotion brought in. At the end of the promotion, total all of the weekly results for a grand total of client responses to this promotion. Be sure to note bad weather, illness, or any mishaps that may have interfered with your promotion's potential success.)

Mother's Day Treat

Every Mother

who has a

service the day before

Mother's Day

receives

a Long Stem Red Rose.

Salon Name
Address
Phone

MOTHER'S DAY PROMOTION

Objective
✂ Treat every mother who is a client to a free rose!

Description
✂ Purchase roses from a wholesale florist to give out the day before Mother's Day.

Preparation
✂ **Two Months Before:** Order flowers (order one for every client you could see on the day before Mother's Day).

Meet with salon staff and explain the promo to everyone.

✂ **Day Before:** Pick up flowers and store in a cool area. Make a poster or flyer of this handout and post it in the salon.

Estimated Cost
✂ $.40-.80 per flower if roses are used.

PROMOTION TRACKING SHEET

(Keep This on a Clipboard at the Reception Desk)

_____

NAME OF PROMOTION

_____   _____

DATE PROMO STARTS   DATE PROMO ENDS

_____

AMOUNT OF NEW CUSTOMERS

	SUN	MON	TUE	WED	THU	FRI	SAT
Week 1							
Week 2							
Week 3							
Week 4							
Monthly Total							

(At the end of every day, take a moment to jot down the number of clients this promotion brought in. At the end of the promotion, total all of the weekly results for a grand total of client responses to this promotion. Be sure to note bad weather, illness, or any mishaps that may have interfered with your promotion's potential success.)

DESERVES A BREAK

A PRICE BREAK

Haircuts Half-Price,
the day before FATHER'S DAY

BOOK YOUR APPOINTMENT NOW

SALON NAME:

Address:

Phone:

Book Your Appointment Now

Selected Stylists Participating

FATHER'S DAY PROMOTION

Objective
✂ Treat every client who is a father to a half-price cut!

Description
✂ Put up a poster and make and distribute flyers.

Preparation
✂ **One Month Before:** Make poster and flyer. Send flyer out to all male clients on mailing list.

Meet with salon staff and explain the promo to everyone.

Estimated Cost
✂ $20 for flyers

PROMOTION TRACKING SHEET

(Keep This on a Clipboard at the Reception Desk)

_____
NAME OF PROMOTION

_____   _____
DATE PROMO STARTS   DATE PROMO ENDS

_____
AMOUNT OF NEW CUSTOMERS

	SUN	MON	TUE	WED	THU	FRI	SAT
Week 1							
Week 2							
Week 3							
Week 4							
Monthly Total							

(At the end of every day, take a moment to jot down the number of clients this promotion brought in. At the end of the promotion, total all of the weekly results for a grand total of client responses to this promotion. Be sure to note bad weather, illness, or any mishaps that may have interfered with your promotion's potential success.)

ASTER BUNNY-BASKET OF SAVINGS

**The
Easter Bunny
Has a Basket of
Savings for You!**

Your Photo Here
You in a Bunny Suit
Holding a Basket

Pick an egg
and receive
the discount
listed inside
the egg!

SALON NAME
Address
Phone

Offer limited to selected stylists, while supplies last.

EASTER BUNNY PROMOTION

Objective
☞ Sell additional services through a discount offer.

Description
☞ Take a photo of yourself in a bunny suit, holding a basket full of eggs, in the salon waiting room.

Preparation
☞ **Two Months Before:** Place an ad in newspaper or make flyers. (Buy neon paper to run flyers on.) Purchase a basket and plastic eggs that you can put slips of paper with different discounts on them.

☞ **One Month Before:** Distribute flyers as bag stuffers. Notify current clients by posting a flyer on your bulletin board for a month previous to the promotion.

Meet with salon staff and explain the promo to everyone. Give all a stack of flyers to distribute.

☞ **One Week Before:** Double check with the newspaper, get a copy of the ad slick, if you have not already done so, and run off flyers on lavender and yellow paper.

☞ **One Day Before the Ad Runs:** Review promo with staff. Make copy of the tracking sheet.

Estimated Cost
☞ $20–30 if only flyers used. Additional cost for newspaper ad—depends on ad size and newspaper rates. Also, remember to allocate funds to rent the bunny suit (an inexpensive alternative is to create a humorous suit from homemade ears, a fluffy tail tacked on long underwear. A male staff member with a beard works best in this outfit!).

PROMOTION TRACKING SHEET

(Keep This on a Clipboard at the Reception Desk)

_____

NAME OF PROMOTION

_____   _____

DATE PROMO STARTS   DATE PROMO ENDS

_____

AMOUNT OF NEW CUSTOMERS

	SUN	MON	TUE	WED	THU	FRI	SAT
Week 1							
Week 2							
Week 3							
Week 4							
Monthly Total							

(At the end of every day, take a moment to jot down the number of clients this promotion brought in. At the end of the promotion, total all of the weekly results for a grand total of client responses to this promotion. Be sure to note bad weather, illness, or any mishaps that may have interfered with your promotion's potential success.)

CHRISTMAS
stocking stuffers

*S*top the holiday madness,

let our staff complete your shopping for you!

*D*uring the month of December, we will offer special

"Holiday Gift Packs and Gift Certificates."

*L*et us wrap a "Stocking" that always fits:

- Gift certificates for a perm and cut
- Glamorous makeup gift packs
- Glittering nail jewelry
- Pedicure and manicure gift certificates

salon name

address

phone

CHRISTMAS STOCKING STUFFER PROMOTION

Objective
✂ Reach new clients. Boost sales pre-holiday.

Description
✂ Buy red stockings and stuff them with retail items and gift certificates for services.

Preparation
✂ **Two Months Before:** Create your own flyer to show off your new holiday look!

✂ **One Month Before:** Distribute flyers as bag stuffers notify current clients by posting a flyer on your bulletin board for a month previous to the promotion.

Meet with salon staff and explain the promo to everyone. Share ideas for a new holiday look. Give all a stack of flyers to distribute.

✂ **One Week Before:** Put up a poster in the salon and set up a retail display.

✂ **One Day Before:** Review promo with staff make copy of the tracking sheet.

Estimated Cost
✂ $20–30 for flyers used. Cost of stockings is minimal. Purchase gift wrap and bows at discount store: about $30.

PROMOTION TRACKING SHEET

(Keep This on a Clipboard at the Reception Desk)

_____

NAME OF PROMOTION

_____   _____

DATE PROMO STARTS   DATE PROMO ENDS

_____

AMOUNT OF NEW CUSTOMERS

	SUN	MON	TUE	WED	THU	FRI	SAT
Week 1							
Week 2							
Week 3							
Week 4							
Monthly Total							

(At the end of every day, take a moment to jot down the number of clients this promotion brought in. At the end of the promotion, total all of the weekly results for a grand total of client responses to this promotion. Be sure to note bad weather, illness, or any mishaps that may have interfered with your promotion's potential success.)

HOLIDAY GLITZ AND GLAMOUR

Makeovers for Holiday Parties!

Don't just buy a new dress and wear the same old hairstyle,
let our salon make you over for your holiday parties.

**During the month of December,
we will offer special
"Holiday Glamour Looks"**

Try Our:
Chic up-dos and party hairstyles
Glamourous make-up applications
Glittering nail art and manicures

SALON NAME:
ADDRESS
PHONE

HOLIDAY GLAMOUR PROMOTION

Objective
ଈ⟨ Reach new clients. Boost sales pre-holiday.

Description
ଈ⟨ Offer new styles and ideas for parties.

Preparation
ଈ⟨ **Two Months Before:** Place an ad in newspaper and get copy of the ad slick to use for flyers. (Buy red and green paper to run flyers on.) Be sure to use a glamour photo or two, that show a fresh, new, holiday look!

ଈ⟨ **One Month Before:** Distribute flyers as bag stuffers. Notify current clients by posting a flyer on your bulletin board for a month previous to the promotion.

Meet with salon staff and explain the promo to everyone. Share ideas for a new holiday look. Give all a stack of flyers to distribute.

ଈ⟨ **One Week Before:** Double check with the newspaper.

ଈ⟨ **One Day Before the Ad Runs:** Review promo with staff. Make copy of the tracking sheet.

Estimated Cost
ଈ⟨ $20-30 if only flyers used. Additional cost for newspaper ad—depends on ad size and newspaper rates.

PROMOTION TRACKING SHEET

(Keep This on a Clipboard at the Reception Desk)

_____

NAME OF PROMOTION

_____   _____

DATE PROMO STARTS   DATE PROMO ENDS

_____

AMOUNT OF NEW CUSTOMERS

	SUN	MON	TUE	WED	THU	FRI	SAT
Week 1							
Week 2							
Week 3							
Week 4							
Monthly Total							

(At the end of every day, take a moment to jot down the number of clients this promotion brought in. At the end of the promotion, total all of the weekly results for a grand total of client responses to this promotion. Be sure to note bad weather, illness, or any mishaps that may have interfered with your promotion's potential success.)

VACATION EXTRAVAGANZA

Take a cool discount off of any service before you pack it in for vacation.

Bring in your tickets, reservations or itinerary along with this Cool-Pon for 10% off any service, on the week before your trip!

10% DISCOUNT OFFER ON ALL "PRE-VACATION" HAIR SERVICES

You Don't Have to be Extravagant to Look Like a MILLION on Vacation

Salon Name

Address
Phone No.

Selected Stylists Only
Offer Expires 10/1/97

VACATION EXTRAVAGANZA PROMOTION

Objective
✂ Reach new clients. Boost sales during vacation.

Description
✂ Offer a discount for a time that is traditionally the slowest time of the year.

Preparation
✂ Create a flyer or have certificates printed up.

✂ **One Month Before**: Distribute flyers as bag stuffers notify current clients by posting a flyer on your bulletin board for a month previous to the promotion.

Meet with salon staff and explain the promo to everyone. Give all a stack of flyers to distribute.

✂ **One Day Before**: Review promo with staff, make copy of the tracking sheet.

Estimated Cost
✂ $20–30 if only flyers used. Additional cost for professional coupons, if used.

PROMOTION
TRACKING SHEET

(Keep This on a Clipboard at the Reception Desk)

_____
NAME OF PROMOTION

_____   _____
DATE PROMO STARTS   DATE PROMO ENDS

_____
AMOUNT OF NEW CUSTOMERS

	SUN	MON	TUE	WED	THU	FRI	SAT
Week 1							
Week 2							
Week 3							
Week 4							
Monthly Total							

(At the end of every day, take a moment to jot down the number of clients this promotion brought in. At the end of the promotion, total all of the weekly results for a grand total of client responses to this promotion. Be sure to note bad weather, illness, or any mishaps that may have interfered with your promotion's potential success.)

THE WET HEAD IS DEAD!!
-FREE DRAWING-
WIN A NEW
PROFESSIONAL HAIRDRYER
(just like hairstylists use)
Date of Drawing
__/__/__
SALON NAME
Address
Phone No.
You don't have to be present to win.
One entry per customer

WET HEAD IS DEAD PROMOTION

Objective
✄ Create a mailing list to use for flyers and sales.

Description
✄ Set up a pretty hat box with a slit in it, and slips of paper to register on. Display the hairdryer.

Preparation
✄ **Two Months Before:** Create your salon's flyer to distribute. Be sure to buy a pretty tablecloth and display the entry box and dryer in a prominent place.

✄ **One Month Before:** Make a sign to go over the entry box. Meet with salon staff and explain the promo to everyone. Share ideas for display table and how to use the mail list to increase business.

✄ **One Day Before:** Review promo with staff, set up table. Make copy of the tracking sheet.

Estimated Cost
✄ $20-30 if only flyers used. Cost of tablecloth and hat box approximately $20, plus cost of hairdryer.

PROMOTION TRACKING SHEET

(Keep This on a Clipboard at the Reception Desk)

_____

NAME OF PROMOTION

_____   _____

DATE PROMO STARTS   DATE PROMO ENDS

_____

AMOUNT OF NEW CUSTOMERS

	SUN	MON	TUE	WED	THU	FRI	SAT
Week 1							
Week 2							
Week 3							
Week 4							
Monthly Total							

(At the end of every day, take a moment to jot down the number of clients this promotion brought in. At the end of the promotion, total all of the weekly results for a grand total of client responses to this promotion. Be sure to note bad weather, illness, or any mishaps that may have interfered with your promotion's potential success.)

ATTENTION: TENNIS FANS

You are cordially invited to our
First Annual
WIMBLEDON SALE

Just tell us the scores from the previous days match and will give you a
10% discount on your haircut!

SALON NAME

ADDRESS PHONE

Selected Stylists Only

SPORTS FANS PROMOTION

Objective
✄ Reach new clients. Boost sales.

Description
✄ Offer a discount during any sports event.

Preparation
✄ **Two Months Before:** Place an ad in newspaper and get copy of the ad slick to use for flyers. (Buy red and green paper to run flyers on.) Be sure to use a sketch or a photo that shows the sport you are featuring.

✄ **One Month Before:** Distribute flyers as bag stuffers. Notify current clients by posting a flyer on your bulletin board for a month previous to the promotion. Secure posters of the sporting event.

Meet with salon staff and explain the promo to everyone. Share ideas for promo. Give all a stack of flyers to distribute. Put up poster.

✄ **One Week Before:** Double check with the newspaper.

✄ **One Day Before the Ad Runs:** Review promo with staff. Make copy of the tracking sheet.

Estimated Cost
✄ $20-30 if only flyers used. Additional cost for newspaper ad—depends on ad size and newspaper rates. Posters cost around $5 each.

PROMOTION TRACKING SHEET

(Keep This on a Clipboard at the Reception Desk)

NAME OF PROMOTION

DATE PROMO STARTS   DATE PROMO ENDS

AMOUNT OF NEW CUSTOMERS

	SUN	MON	TUE	WED	THU	FRI	SAT
Week 1							
Week 2							
Week 3							
Week 4							
Monthly Total							

(At the end of every day, take a moment to jot down the number of clients this promotion brought in. At the end of the promotion, total all of the weekly results for a grand total of client responses to this promotion. Be sure to note bad weather, illness, or any mishaps that may have interfered with your promotion's potential success.)

This month, kin-folk get 2 haircuts fer the price of 1.

EVERY MONDAY

Salon Name
Address
Phone

C'mon in fer the 2 fer sale in July pull up a rockin' chair, set a while and visit with us around the pickle barrel.

Y'all come back now, Y'hear!

SELECTED STYLISTS
Offer Ends July 30th

2 FER PROMOTION

Objective
✂ Reach new clients. Boost summer sales.

Description
✂ Offer a free cut with a cut purchased for a relative.

Preparation
✂ **Two Months Before:** Place an ad in newspaper and get copy of the ad slick to use for flyers. (Buy bright paper to run flyers on.) Secure a pickle barrel and two rocking chairs; perhaps a bale of hay instead of the barrel.

✂ **One Month Before:** Distribute flyers as bag stuffers. Notify current clients by posting a flyer on your bulletin board for a month previous to the promotion.

Meet with salon staff and explain the promo to everyone. Share ideas for a fun look, perhaps everyone wears coveralls on Mondays. Give all a stack of flyers to distribute.

✂ **One Week Before:** Double check with the newspaper.

✂ **One Day Before the Ad Runs:** Review promo with staff. Make copy of the tracking sheet. Set up barrel and chairs.

Estimated Cost
✂ $20-30 if only flyers used. Additional cost for newspaper ad—depends on ad size and newspaper rates. Cost of chairs and barrel depend on area. Try yard sales and thrift stores.

PROMOTION TRACKING SHEET

(Keep This on a Clipboard at the Reception Desk)

NAME OF PROMOTION

DATE PROMO STARTS   DATE PROMO ENDS

AMOUNT OF NEW CUSTOMERS

	SUN	MON	TUE	WED	THU	FRI	SAT
Week 1							
Week 2							
Week 3							
Week 4							
Monthly Total							

(At the end of every day, take a moment to jot down the number of clients this promotion brought in. At the end of the promotion, total all of the weekly results for a grand total of client responses to this promotion. Be sure to note bad weather, illness, or any mishaps that may have interfered with your promotion's potential success.)

SISTERS SAVE MONEY!

This week only...
Treat your sister to a free haircut when
you purchase your cut!

*Give her a call,
come in together
and cut the
cost of haircuts
in half.*

SALON NAME
Address
Phone

SELECTED STYLISTS ONLY
April 10 to 17 Only

SISTERS SAVE PROMOTION

Objective

✂ Reach new clients. Boost sales.

Description

✂ Offer a free cut for her sister, to anyone who buys one haircut at the regular price.

Preparation

✂ **Two Months Before:** Place an ad in the newspaper and get copies of the ad slick to use for flyers. (Buy colored paper to run flyers on.)

✂ **One Month Before:** Distribute flyers as bag stuffers. Notify current clients by posting a flyer on your bulletin board for a month previous to the promotion.

Meet with salon staff and explain the promo to everyone. Give all a stack of flyers to distribute.

✂ **One Week Before:** Double check with the newspaper.

✂ **One Day Before the Ad Runs:** Review promo with staff. Make copy of the tracking sheet.

Estimated Cost

✂ $20-30 if only flyers used. Additional cost for newspaper ad—depends on ad size and newspaper rates.

PROMOTION TRACKING SHEET

(Keep This on a Clipboard at the Reception Desk)

_____

NAME OF PROMOTION

_____   _____

DATE PROMO STARTS   DATE PROMO ENDS

_____

AMOUNT OF NEW CUSTOMERS

	SUN	MON	TUE	WED	THU	FRI	SAT
Week 1							
Week 2							
Week 3							
Week 4							
Monthly Total							

(At the end of every day, take a moment to jot down the number of clients this promotion brought in. At the end of the promotion, total all of the weekly results for a grand total of client responses to this promotion. Be sure to note bad weather, illness, or any mishaps that may have interfered with your promotion's potential success.)

CUT-A-THON

on

May 10, 1998
10 am to 5 pm

Westchester Mall

Sponsored by:

SALON NAME

Address
Phone

All proceeds to benefit Hospice of New York.
No appointments taken, just show up.
All haircuts $9.00. Get a great haircut and
help a great charity.

CUT-A-THON PROMOTION

Objective

✂ Reach new clients. Earn $ for your favorite charity.

Description

✂ Offer a sale price and give all the money to charity.

Preparation

✂ **Two Months Before**: Contact a charity and find out what they can do to help you with the cut-a-thon. Be sure they are there to collect the money for you. Place an ad in newspaper and get a copy of the ad slick to use for flyers. (Buy paper to run flyers on.) Be sure to use a glamour photo or two, that show a fresh, new look! Send a press release to all TV, radio and newspapers.

✂ **One Month Before**: Distribute flyers as bag stuffers. Notify current clients by posting a flyer on your bulletin board for a month previous to the promotion.

Meet with salon staff and explain the promo to everyone. Give all a stack of flyers to distribute.

✂ **One Week Before**: Double check with the newspaper.

✂ **One Day Before the Ad Runs**: Review promo with staff. Make copy of the tracking sheet.

Estimated Cost

✂ $20–30 if only flyers used. Additional cost for newspaper ad—depends on ad size and newspaper rates.

PROMOTION
TRACKING SHEET

(Keep This on a Clipboard at the Reception Desk)

_____
NAME OF PROMOTION

_____   _____
DATE PROMO STARTS   DATE PROMO ENDS

_____
AMOUNT OF NEW CUSTOMERS

	SUN	MON	TUE	WED	THU	FRI	SAT
Week 1							
Week 2							
Week 3							
Week 4							
Monthly Total							

(At the end of every day, take a moment to jot down the number of clients this promotion brought in. At the end of the promotion, total all of the weekly results for a grand total of client responses to this promotion. Be sure to note bad weather, illness, or any mishaps that may have interfered with your promotion's potential success.)

BUTTONS, BUTTONS, BUTTONS PROMOTION

Objective
✂ Reach new clients. Boost sales with teens and kids.

Description
✂ Offer a free button for clients to wear and collect.

Preparation
✂ **Two Months Before**: Decide on a cute logo and order buttons for clients to wear. Check with screen printers and copy stores. Get a few samples to display in the salon.

✂ **One Month Before**: Display a piece of fabric with your buttons all over it!

Meet with salon staff and explain the promo to everyone.

✂ **One Week Before**: Double check with button manufacturer or screen printer. Be sure they will be ready on time.

✂ **One Day Before**: Review promo with staff. Make copy of the tracking sheet.

Estimated Cost
✂ Buttons—get estimates—buttons should cost less than a dollar each.

PROMOTION TRACKING SHEET

Keep This on a Clipboard at the Reception Desk)

_____

NAME OF PROMOTION

_____   _____

DATE PROMO STARTS   DATE PROMO ENDS

_____

AMOUNT OF NEW CUSTOMERS

	SUN	MON	TUE	WED	THU	FRI	SAT
Week 1							
Week 2							
Week 3							
Week 4							
Monthly Total							

(At the end of every day, take a moment to jot down the number of clients this promotion brought in. At the end of the promotion, total all of the weekly results for a grand total of client responses to this promotion. Be sure to note bad weather, illness, or any mishaps that may have interfered with your promotion's potential success.)

BACK TO SCHOOL STICKERS

Salon Name
Address
Phone No.

is proud to offer you—

FREE! FREE! FREE! FREE!

Back to School Stickers

for our customers
under 12 years of age

Hurry in...limited quantities

BACK TO SCHOOL STICKERS PROMOTION

Objective
&< Reach new clients. Boost sales with kids and parents.

Description
&< Offer free stickers for kids to wear and collect. Put salon logo and a "no drugs" message on them.

Preparation
&< **Two Months Before:** Decide on a cute logo and order stickers from photo stores. Get a few samples to display in the salon. (Charities like "MADD" will help you distribute them.)

&< **One Month Before:** Display a piece of poster board with your stickers all over it!

Meet with salon staff and explain the promo to everyone.

&< **One Week Before:** Double check with sticker manufacture. Be sure they will be ready on time. Contact schools in the area and offer to give them out free!

&< **One Day Before:** Review promo with staff. Make copy of the tracking sheet.

Estimated Cost
&< Stickers—get estimates—stickers should cost less than $.25 each.

PROMOTION
TRACKING SHEET

(Keep This on a Clipboard at the Reception Desk)

_____

NAME OF PROMOTION

_____   _____

DATE PROMO STARTS   DATE PROMO ENDS

_____

AMOUNT OF NEW CUSTOMERS

	SUN	MON	TUE	WED	THU	FRI	SAT
Week 1							
Week 2							
Week 3							
Week 4							
Monthly Total							

(At the end of every day, take a moment to jot down the number of clients this promotion brought in. At the end of the promotion, total all of the weekly results for a grand total of client responses to this promotion. Be sure to note bad weather, illness, or any mishaps that may have interfered with your promotion's potential success.)

New Pens
for
New Neighbors!

Salon

*Welcome
to the
Neighborhood*

Staff Photo
Here

Salon Name
address
phone

NEW PENS FOR NEW NEIGHBORS PROMOTION

Objective
✄ Reach new clients.

Description
✄ Offer a free pen for clients who are new to area.

Preparation
✄ Decide on a cute logo and order pens. (Check with a screen printer and copy stores.) Contact welcome wagon and give them the pens to distribute for you.

Meet with salon staff and explain the promo to everyone.

Estimated Cost
✄ Pens—get estimates—but should cost less than $.50 each.

PROMOTION TRACKING SHEET

(keep This on a Clipboard at the Reception Desk)

_____

NAME OF PROMOTION

_____   _____

DATE PROMO STARTS   DATE PROMO ENDS

_____

AMOUNT OF NEW CUSTOMERS

	SUN	MON	TUE	WED	THU	FRI	SAT
Week 1							
Week 2							
Week 3							
Week 4							
Monthly Total							

(At the end of every day, take a moment to jot down the number of clients this promotion brought in. At the end of the promotion, total all of the weekly results for a grand total of client responses to this promotion. Be sure to note bad weather, illness, or any mishaps that may have interfered with your promotion's potential success.)

AN ISLAND ESCAPE FOR YOU

Escape to our Island of Relaxation with a Day of Pampering

SALON NAME

**Is proud to offer you an Island Escape Day!
Let us surround you in waves of luxurious pampering.**

We will:
- ☆ **cruise you through a facial and body massage**
- ☆ **drape you in luxury with a manicure and pedicure**
- ☆ **romance you with a new hairstyle**
- ☆ **lunch will be served on a silver platter and you will be chauffeured to and from your appointment by our driver**

Appointments are limited, so call and book yours today.

There will be no stress left after your Island Escape.

WE GUARANTEE IT!

Salon Name
Address
Phone

ISLAND ESCAPE PROMOTION

Objective
✂ Reach new clients. Boost sales with upscale promo.

Description
✂ Offer a day of pampering to clients.

Preparation
✂ **Two Months Before:** Choose a newspaper ad.

✂ **One Month Before:** Make arrangements for lunch on a silver platter, a staff member to drive the clients, meet with salon staff and explain the promo to everyone. This is a very upscale promotion and you will be able to price it dearly, but you must synchronize it and be sure the service is impeccable.

Make engraved invitations and mail them out to mailing list.

✂ **One Week Before:** Double check with newspaper, proof ad.

✂ **One Day Before:** Review promo with staff. Make copy of the tracking sheet.

Estimated Cost
✂ Newspaper ad and lunch—get estimates from several sources, prices vary in each city. Also postage expense.

PROMOTION TRACKING SHEET

(Keep This on a Clipboard at the Reception Desk)

_____

NAME OF PROMOTION

_____   _____

DATE PROMO STARTS   DATE PROMO ENDS

_____

AMOUNT OF NEW CUSTOMERS

	SUN	MON	TUE	WED	THU	FRI	SAT
Week 1							
Week 2							
Week 3							
Week 4							
Monthly Total							

(At the end of every day, take a moment to jot down the number of clients this promotion brought in. At the end of the promotion, total all of the weekly results for a grand total of client responses to this promotion. Be sure to note bad weather, illness, or any mishaps that may have interfered with your promotion's potential success.)

SINGLES MINGLE

This Thursday Night, Sept. 2, 1997

Salon Name
Will hold it's first

SINGLES MINGLE!
From 6 to 10 pm
All single clients are welcome to come

HALF PRICE HAIRCUTS!

Refreshments Served

Come and meet other singles
and get a great sale price!

SALON NAME
PHONE

SINGLES MINGLE PROMOTION

Objective
ぅ━Reach new clients. Boost sales.

Description
ぅ━Offer a place to meet other singles and half-price cuts.

Preparation
ぅ━**Two Months Before**: Make a flyer and distribute to singles clubs, groups, Sunday schools, apartment communities, etc.

Meet with salon staff and explain the promo to everyone. Arrange for refreshments.

ぅ━**One Week Before**: Double check with refreshments.

ぅ━**One Day Before**: Review promo with staff. Make copy of the tracking sheet.

Estimated Cost
ぅ━Flyers $20–30 and refreshments (chips, sub sandwiches, cola, pizza; price varies in your town, so comparison shop).

PROMOTION TRACKING SHEET

(Keep This on a Clipboard at the Reception Desk)

_____

NAME OF PROMOTION

_____   _____

DATE PROMO STARTS   DATE PROMO ENDS

_____

AMOUNT OF NEW CUSTOMERS

	SUN	MON	TUE	WED	THU	FRI	SAT
Week 1							
Week 2							
Week 3							
Week 4							
Monthly Total							

(At the end of every day, take a moment to jot down the number of clients this promotion brought in. At the end of the promotion, total all of the weekly results for a grand total of client responses to this promotion. Be sure to note bad weather, illness, or any mishaps that may have interfered with your promotion's potential success.)

NASCAR SALE RACE IN FOR SAVINGS

This Sunday Afternoon During The NASCAR Race,
Purchase a Haircut at the Regular Price
and

THE FINISH IS ON US!!

SALON NAME

ADDRESS

PHONE

SELECTED STYLISTS

THE FINISH IS ON US PROMOTION

Objective

✂ Reach new clients. Boost sales.

Description

✂ Offer a free style, set, or blow-dry during the race with purchase of a cut.

Preparation

✂ **One Month Before**: Make a flyer and distribute to singles clubs, groups, Sunday schools, apartment communities, etc.

Meet with salon staff and explain the promo to everyone. Arrange for checkered flags, race driver posters and picture cards.

✂ **One Day Before**: Review promo with staff. Make copy of the tracking sheet.

Estimated Cost

✂ Flags $5–10 and flyers $20. Posters and cards $10. Visit toy department and sports department of discount stores for props to put around the salon.

PROMOTION TRACKING SHEET

(Keep This on a Clipboard at the Reception Desk)

_____

NAME OF PROMOTION

_____   _____

DATE PROMO STARTS   DATE PROMO ENDS

_____

AMOUNT OF NEW CUSTOMERS

	SUN	MON	TUE	WED	THU	FRI	SAT
Week 1							
Week 2							
Week 3							
Week 4							
Monthly Total							

(At the end of every day, take a moment to jot down the number of clients this promotion brought in. At the end of the promotion, total all of the weekly results for a grand total of client responses to this promotion. Be sure to note bad weather, illness, or any mishaps that may have interfered with your promotion's potential success.)

DOG DAYS OF SUMMER SALE

Spend those sultry afternoons in our cool salon and

Beat the Heat with

A REAL COOL DEAL

Half-Price Perms

with Selected Stylists

SALON NAME
Address
Phone No.

Offer Expires August 28, 1998

DOG DAYS OF SUMMER PROMOTION

Objective
✄ Reach new clients. Boost sales.

Description
✄ Offer a place to beat the heat and get a sale perm.

Preparation
✄ **Two Months Before:** Make a flyer and distribute to clubs, groups, Sunday schools, apartments, etc. (Great flyer to use: a photo of your dog and you.)

Meet with salon staff and explain the promo to everyone.

✄ **One Day Before:** Review promo with staff. Make copy of the tracking sheet.

Estimated Cost
✄ Flyers $20–30

PROMOTION TRACKING SHEET

(Keep This on a Clipboard at the Reception Desk)

_____

NAME OF PROMOTION

_____   _____

DATE PROMO STARTS   DATE PROMO ENDS

_____

AMOUNT OF NEW CUSTOMERS

	SUN	MON	TUE	WED	THU	FRI	SAT
Week 1							
Week 2							
Week 3							
Week 4							
Monthly Total							

(At the end of every day, take a moment to jot down the number of clients this promotion brought in. At the end of the promotion, total all of the weekly results for a grand total of client responses to this promotion. Be sure to note bad weather, illness, or any mishaps that may have interfered with your promotion's potential success.)

COLOR

Try It On

At an introductory price, try the color
you always dreamed you could be...

TRY ANY COLOR
FOR $30.00

Photo of a
blond, brunette and Redhead

SEE COLOR MFG.
FOR FREE PHOTO

SIZZLING BLONDES

BRILLIANT REDHEADS

DAZZLING BRUNETTES

Salon Name
Address
Phone

SELECTED SALONS ONLY • OFFER EXPIRES JULY 1, 1997

TRY IT ON PROMOTION

Objective
✃Reach new clients. Boost color sales.

Description
✃Offer an introductory price on color.

Preparation
✃**Two Months Before:** Make a flyer and distribute to singles clubs, groups, Sunday schools, apartment communities, etc. Mail it to client list. Post one in the salon—note a start date on it.

Call your beauty supply and color manufacturer, will they help with co-op ad money or donate color?

Meet with salon staff and explain the promo to everyone. Arrange for extra color photos.

✃**One Week Before:** Double check color supplies.

✃**One Day Before:** Review promo with staff. Make copy of the tracking sheet.

Estimated Cost
✃Flyers $20-30 and postage if mailing is done.

PROMOTION TRACKING SHEET

(Keep This on a Clipboard at the Reception Desk)

_____

NAME OF PROMOTION

_____   _____

DATE PROMO STARTS   DATE PROMO ENDS

_____

AMOUNT OF NEW CUSTOMERS

	SUN	MON	TUE	WED	THU	FRI	SAT
Week 1							
Week 2							
Week 3							
Week 4							
Monthly Total							

(At the end of every day, take a moment to jot down the number of clients this promotion brought in. At the end of the promotion, total all of the weekly results for a grand total of client responses to this promotion. Be sure to note bad weather, illness, or any mishaps that may have interfered with your promotion's potential success.)

SUPERBOWL WIDOW'S SPECIAL OFFER

While he watches the Superbowl and
ignores you...

Your best friend and you are invited
to our salon for an afternoon of fun

- **A Hair Show of Latest Styles**
- **A Chocolate Dessert to End All Desserts**
- **A Drawing for a Wonderful Door Prize**

SALON NAME
Address
Phone No.

SUPERBOWL WIDOW PROMOTION

Objective
✂ Reach new clients. Boost sales.

Description
✂ Offer an afternoon hair show and fun on a day she is traditionally looking for something to do!

Preparation
✂ **Two Months Before:** Make a flyer and distribute to women's clubs, groups, Sunday schools, apartment communities, etc. Mail it to client list. Post one in the salon.

Meet with salon staff and explain the promo to everyone. Get volunteers to create styles for the hair show. Arrange for chocolate desserts.

✂ **One Week Before:** Double check with staff on styles.

✂ **One Day Before:** Review promo with staff, pick up dessert. Make copy of the tracking sheet.

Estimated Cost
✂ $20-30 and postage if mailing is done. Dessert—$25 approx.

PROMOTION TRACKING SHEET

(Keep This on a Clipboard at the Reception Desk)

_____

NAME OF PROMOTION

_____   _____

DATE PROMO STARTS   DATE PROMO ENDS

_____

AMOUNT OF NEW CUSTOMERS

	SUN	MON	TUE	WED	THU	FRI	SAT
Week 1							
Week 2							
Week 3							
Week 4							
Monthly Total							

(At the end of every day, take a moment to jot down the number of clients this promotion brought in. At the end of the promotion, total all of the weekly results for a grand total of client responses to this promotion. Be sure to note bad weather, illness, or any mishaps that may have interfered with your promotion's potential success.)

Place an Ad in the Local Newspaper, But...

Have the Newspaper print it **UPSIDE DOWN,** so that the reader has to turn the paper upside down to read your ad.

See how effective this is!

UPSIDE DOWN AD/PROMOTION

Objective

- Reach new clients.

Description

- Offer a sale on a service or place an ad in the newspaper.

Preparation

- **Two Months Before:** Place an ad in newspaper. Be sure they know you have to place the ad upside down to draw attention to it.

  Meet with salon staff and explain the promo to everyone. Give all a stack of flyers to distribute.

- **One Week Before:** Double check with the newspaper.

- **One Day Before the Ad Runs:** Review promo with staff. Make copy of the tracking sheet.

Estimated Cost

- Newspaper ad—depends on ad size and newspaper rates.

PROMOTION TRACKING SHEET

(Keep This on a Clipboard at the Reception Desk)

_____

NAME OF PROMOTION

_____   _____

DATE PROMO STARTS   DATE PROMO ENDS

_____

AMOUNT OF NEW CUSTOMERS

	SUN	MON	TUE	WED	THU	FRI	SAT
Week 1							
Week 2							
Week 3							
Week 4							
Monthly Total							

(At the end of every day, take a moment to jot down the number of clients this promotion brought in. At the end of the promotion, total all of the weekly results for a grand total of client responses to this promotion. Be sure to note bad weather, illness, or any mishaps that may have interfered with your promotion's potential success.)

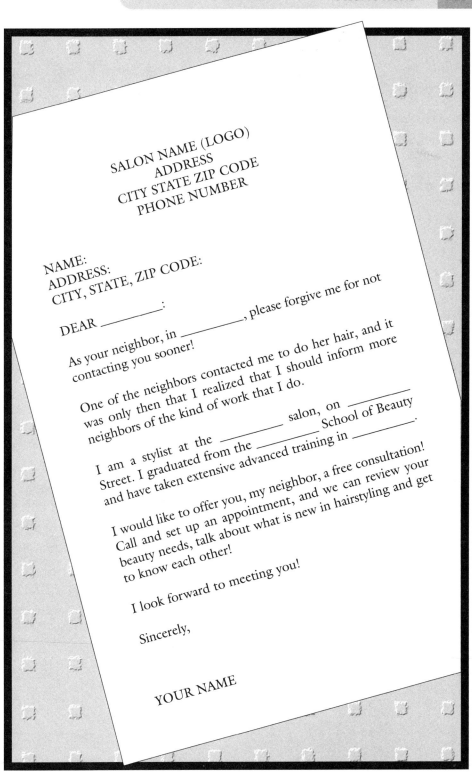

SALON NAME (LOGO)
ADDRESS
CITY STATE ZIP CODE
PHONE NUMBER

NAME:
ADDRESS:
CITY, STATE, ZIP CODE:

DEAR _____:

As your neighbor, in _____, please forgive me for not contacting you sooner!

One of the neighbors contacted me to do her hair, and it was only then that I realized that I should inform more neighbors of the kind of work that I do.

I am a stylist at the _____ salon, on _____ Street. I graduated from the _____ School of Beauty and have taken extensive advanced training in _____.

I would like to offer you, my neighbor, a free consultation! Call and set up an appointment, and we can review your beauty needs, talk about what is new in hairstyling and get to know each other!

I look forward to meeting you!

Sincerely,

YOUR NAME

NEW TO NEIGHBORHOOD PROMOTION

Objective
✂ Reach new clients.

Description
✂ Offer a free consultation to neighbors.

Preparation
✂ Meet with salon staff and explain the promo to everyone.

✂ **One Week Before:** Write letters and get a street directory from the local library. Make a mailing list from it.

✂ **One Day Before:** Make copy of the tracking sheet.

Estimated Cost
✂ $20–30 if only letters used. Additional cost for postage.

PROMOTION TRACKING SHEET

(Keep This on a Clipboard at the Reception Desk)

_____

NAME OF PROMOTION

_____   _____

DATE PROMO STARTS   DATE PROMO ENDS

_____

AMOUNT OF NEW CUSTOMERS

	SUN	MON	TUE	WED	THU	FRI	SAT
Week 1							
Week 2							
Week 3							
Week 4							
Monthly Total							

(At the end of every day, take a moment to jot down the number of clients this promotion brought in. At the end of the promotion, total all of the weekly results for a grand total of client responses to this promotion. Be sure to note bad weather, illness, or any mishaps that may have interfered with your promotion's potential success.)

A MASTERFUL CUT FOR THE YOUNG MASTER

WE SPECIALIZE IN CUTS FOR
YOUR YOUNG MASTER

BRING YOUR YOUNG MAN INTO OUR SALON
FOR HIS HAIRCUTS AND...

PAY ONLY $1 FOR EVERY YEAR OF HIS AGE
(TWO YEAR OLDS PAY $2 ETC.)

Call for an Appointment

SALON NAME Address Address **P H O N E**

MASTERFUL CUTS FOR YOUNG MASTERS PROMOTION

Objective
✂ Reach new clients.

Description
✂ Offer a discount price cut for young boys.

Preparation
✂ **Two Months Before:** Place an ad in newspaper and get copy of the ad slick to use for flyers. (Buy neon paper to run flyers on.)

✂ **One Month Before:** Distribute flyers as bag stuffers (children's stores, schools, etc.). Notify current clients by posting a flyer on your bulletin board for a month previous to the promotion.

Meet with salon staff and explain the promo to everyone. Give all a stack of flyers to distribute.

✂ **One Week Before:** Double check with the newspaper, mail flyers to client mailing list.

✂ **One Day Before the Ad Runs:** Review promo with staff. Make copy of the tracking sheet.

Estimated Cost
✂ $20-30 if only flyers used. Additional cost for newspaper ad—depends on ad size and newspaper rates. Also, postage if mailers used.

PROMOTION TRACKING SHEET

(Keep This on a Clipboard at the Reception Desk)

_____

NAME OF PROMOTION

_____   _____

DATE PROMO STARTS   DATE PROMO ENDS

_____

AMOUNT OF NEW CUSTOMERS

	SUN	MON	TUE	WED	THU	FRI	SAT
Week 1							
Week 2							
Week 3							
Week 4							
Monthly Total							

(At the end of every day, take a moment to jot down the number of clients this promotion brought in. At the end of the promotion, total all of the weekly results for a grand total of client responses to this promotion. Be sure to note bad weather, illness, or any mishaps that may have interfered with your promotion's potential success.)

Little Girl's Birthday Party

Ms_____

invites you to
A Birthday "Beauty" Party
to be held at:

Salon Name
Address
Phone No.

What FUN!
Each guest will have a manicure
and her hair French braided.

Date   /   /
Time_____ am

Regrets: 555 -1234

LITTLE GIRL'S BIRTHDAY PARTY PROMOTION

Objective
✂ Reach new clients.

Description
✂ Clients can have their daughter's birthday party in your salon.

Preparation
✂ **Two Months Before:** Provide invitations—book off time for every stylist to do a child's hair and mini manicure.

✂ **One Month Before:** Meet with salon staff and explain the promo to everyone.

✂ **One Week Before:** Double check with child's parent.

✂ **One Day Before:** Review promo with staff. Make copy of the tracking sheet.

Estimated Cost
✂ $2 if only flyers used.

PROMOTION TRACKING SHEET

(Keep This on a Clipboard at the Reception Desk)

_____
NAME OF PROMOTION

_____   _____
DATE PROMO STARTS   DATE PROMO ENDS

_____
AMOUNT OF NEW CUSTOMERS

	SUN	MON	TUE	WED	THU	FRI	SAT
Week 1							
Week 2							
Week 3							
Week 4							
Monthly Total							

(At the end of every day, take a moment to jot down the number of clients this promotion brought in. At the end of the promotion, total all of the weekly results for a grand total of client responses to this promotion. Be sure to note bad weather, illness, or any mishaps that may have interfered with your promotion's potential success.)

Pick the Discount
From
Our Tree

SALON NAME
Address
Phone

Pick a Slip and Get The Discount It Says

YOU PICK THE DISCOUNT PROMOTION

Objective
❀ Reach new clients.

Description
❀ Offer a discount slip from a tree branch that you have taped little colored pieces of paper on. Each one has a discount on it.

Preparation
❀ **One Month Before:** Notify current clients by posting a flyer on your bulletin board for a month previous to the promotion.

Meet with salon staff and explain the promo to everyone.

❀ **One Week Before:** Make the "tree" and discount slips.

❀ **One Day Before:** Review promo with staff. Make copy of the tracking sheet.

Estimated Cost
❀ $1 for paper slips. Take a tree branch and stick it in a vase. Put it on a pretty tablecloth!

PROMOTION TRACKING SHEET

(Keep This on a Clipboard at the Reception Desk)

_____

NAME OF PROMOTION

_____   _____

DATE PROMO STARTS   DATE PROMO ENDS

_____

AMOUNT OF NEW CUSTOMERS

	SUN	MON	TUE	WED	THU	FRI	SAT
Week 1							
Week 2							
Week 3							
Week 4							
Monthly Total							

(At the end of every day, take a moment to jot down the number of clients this promotion brought in. At the end of the promotion, total all of the weekly results for a grand total of client responses to this promotion. Be sure to note bad weather, illness, or any mishaps that may have interfered with your promotion's potential success.)

We Need Models or People Who Would Like to be Models

Salon Name

Address

This Monday Only
We need models for a photo shoot.
We are preparing our portfolio.

If you have what it takes, you could be our model!

Call 555-1212

Ask for Ann

WE NEED MODELS PROMOTION

Objective
✁Reach new clients and create a portfolio for yourself.

Description
✁Offer a free shampoo and style to several who show up for the model search. Reach several new clients with your makeover suggestions; take Polaroids of your work. Book appointments for color and perms for models that choose to purchase additional services.

Preparation
✁**Two Months Before:** Place an ad in newspaper and get copy of the ad slick to use for flyers. (Buy neon paper to run flyers on.)

✁**One Month Before:** Distribute flyers as bag stuffers (stores, resorts, offices, schools). Notify current clients by posting a flyer on your bulletin board for a month previous to the promotion.

Meet with salon staff and explain the promo to everyone. Give all a stack of flyers to distribute

✁**One Week Before:** Double check with the newspaper.

✁**One Day Before the Ad Runs:** Review promo with staff. Make copy of the tracking sheet. Buy film!

Estimated Cost
✁$20-30 if only flyers used. Additional cost for newspaper ad—depends on ad size and newspaper rates. Film—cost varies.

Note: Be sure to serve soft drinks, have lots of staff members around to talk to potential clients, even the ones you turn down.

PROMOTION
TRACKING SHEET

(Keep This on a Clipboard at the Reception Desk)

_____

NAME OF PROMOTION

_____   _____

DATE PROMO STARTS   DATE PROMO ENDS

_____

AMOUNT OF NEW CUSTOMERS

	SUN	MON	TUE	WED	THU	FRI	SAT
Week 1							
Week 2							
Week 3							
Week 4							
Monthly Total							

(At the end of every day, take a moment to jot down the number of clients this promotion brought in. At the end of the promotion, total all of the weekly results for a grand total of client responses to this promotion. Be sure to note bad weather, illness, or any mishaps that may have interfered with your promotion's potential success.)

100,000 MILE OVERHAUL

Salon Name•Phone

We will honor your
frequent flyer points from
any airline.

- Worn out from your hectic travel schedule?

- Suffering from jet lag?

Let us refresh and reward you!

Just bring in your mileage statement.

Mileage Required	Reward You May Request
100,000 Miles	1/2 Price Haircut
125,000 Miles	1/2 Price Haircut and Finish
150,000 Miles	1/2 Price Color and Finish
200,000 Miles	1/2 Price Perm and Finish

Redeemed on Mondays only, with selected stylists

100,000 MILE OVERHAUL PROMOTION

Objective
✂Refresh and reward frequent flyer customers.

Description
✂Offer customers a reward for being a client. Refresh weary traveling clients.

Preparation
✂**Two Months Before:** Create your salon's flyer.

✂**One Month Before:** Distribute flyers as direct mail pieces and send to all airlines in your city—ask them to post one for you.

Meet with salon staff and explain the promo to everyone. Give all a stack of flyers to distribute.

✂**One Day Before:** Review promo with staff. Make copy of the tracking sheet.

Estimated Cost
✂$20-30 if only flyers used. Additional cost for postage.

PROMOTION TRACKING SHEET

(Keep This on a Clipboard at the Reception Desk)

_____

NAME OF PROMOTION

_____   _____

DATE PROMO STARTS   DATE PROMO ENDS

_____

AMOUNT OF NEW CUSTOMERS

	SUN	MON	TUE	WED	THU	FRI	SAT
Week 1							
Week 2							
Week 3							
Week 4							
Monthly Total							

(At the end of every day, take a moment to jot down the number of clients this promotion brought in. At the end of the promotion, total all of the weekly results for a grand total of client responses to this promotion. Be sure to note bad weather, illness, or any mishaps that may have interfered with your promotion's potential success.)

IT'S A SWEETHEART OF A SALE

Just because you are our sweetheart...
We are offering you a
sweet deal!

Have a haircut with us and
your sweetheart gets one free!

Salon Name
Address
Phone

Selected Stylists.
Offer Expires 2/20/98

A SWEETHEART OF A SALE PROMOTION

Objective
8< Reach new haircut clients.

Description
8< Offer a free haircut for your sweetheart, when you have a haircut in our salon, this week only.

Preparation
8< Create your salon's flyer (use pink paper).

8< **One Month Before:** Mail flyers to current client list. Meet with salon staff and explain the promo to everyone. Give all a stack of flyers to distribute.

8< **One Day Before Runs:** Review promo with staff. Make copy of the tracking sheet.

Estimated Cost
8< $20-30 if only flyers used. Additional cost for postage if mailed out.

PROMOTION TRACKING SHEET

(Keep This on a Clipboard at the Reception Desk)

_____

NAME OF PROMOTION

_____   _____

DATE PROMO STARTS   DATE PROMO ENDS

_____

AMOUNT OF NEW CUSTOMERS

	SUN	MON	TUE	WED	THU	FRI	SAT
Week 1							
Week 2							
Week 3							
Week 4							
Monthly Total							

(At the end of every day, take a moment to jot down the number of clients this promotion brought in. At the end of the promotion, total all of the weekly results for a grand total of client responses to this promotion. Be sure to note bad weather, illness, or any mishaps that may have interfered with your promotion's potential success.)

LOCAL TEAM CHAMPS ARE CHAMPIONS WITH US!

Salon Name
Address•Phone

CONGRATULATES YOUR TEAM ON ITS SUCCESS

Bring in this coupon for a
FREE GIFT!!

TEAM NAME HERE

Supplies Limited
Team players only

CHAMPIONS PROMOTION

Objective

≫—Reach new clients. Help support the local sports heroes.

Description

≫—Offer a free gift (comb, nail file, etc.) to the winning local team.

Preparation

≫—**Two Weeks Before:** Meet with salon staff and explain the promo to everyone. Give all a stack of flyers to distribute.

≫—**One Day Before:** Review promo with staff. Make copy of the tracking sheet. Mail out the flyers to the local heroes.

Estimated Cost

≫—$20-30 if only flyers used. Additional cost for gifts (see the sale bin at local beauty supply). Postage for one letter (mailed to team captain or school coach).

PROMOTION TRACKING SHEET

(Keep This on a Clipboard at the Reception Desk)

_____

NAME OF PROMOTION

_____   _____

DATE PROMO STARTS   DATE PROMO ENDS

_____

AMOUNT OF NEW CUSTOMERS

	SUN	MON	TUE	WED	THU	FRI	SAT
Week 1							
Week 2							
Week 3							
Week 4							
Monthly Total							

(At the end of every day, take a moment to jot down the number of clients this promotion brought in. At the end of the promotion, total all of the weekly results for a grand total of client responses to this promotion. Be sure to note bad weather, illness, or any mishaps that may have interfered with your promotion's potential success.)

HOT HAIRCUTS
COOL PRICES

July
Haircut Sale!

Come in for some
HOT NEW LOOKS
in HAIRCUTS
at very cool prices!

All haircuts $20 during the "Cool Prices" sale.
Walk-in customers only at sale price.

Salon Name

Address
Phone No.

HOT HAIRCUTS—COOL PRICES PROMOTION

Objective
✂ Reach new clients.

Description
✂ Offer a free haircut at reduced prices during your slowest month.

Preparation
✂ **One Month Before**: Make and distribute flyers to swimsuit stores, resorts, beach, hotels, schools. Notify current clients by posting a flyer on your bulletin board for a month previous to the promotion.

Meet with salon staff and explain the promo to everyone. Give all a stack of flyers to distribute.

✂ **One Day Before**: Review promo with staff. Make copy of the tracking sheet.

Estimated Cost
✂ $20–30 if only flyers used.

PROMOTION TRACKING SHEET

(Keep This on a Clipboard at the Reception Desk)

_____

NAME OF PROMOTION

_____   _____

DATE PROMO STARTS   DATE PROMO ENDS

_____

AMOUNT OF NEW CUSTOMERS

	SUN	MON	TUE	WED	THU	FRI	SAT
Week 1							
Week 2							
Week 3							
Week 4							
Monthly Total							

(At the end of every day, take a moment to jot down the number of clients this promotion brought in. At the end of the promotion, total all of the weekly results for a grand total of client responses to this promotion. Be sure to note bad weather, illness, or any mishaps that may have interfered with your promotion's potential success.)

CONTEST

Name our Newest Hairstyle and WIN

FREE HAIRCUTS FOR A YEAR!

SALON NAME
ADDRESS
PHONE

When you are here for a service look at the photos of our latest creation and name the style.

One entry per client at point of purchase only.

We have tried and tried but we can't come up with a winning name...can you?

NAME OUR NEW STYLE PROMOTION

Objective
%< Reach clients who have not been in for a while with a new style to entice them.

Description
%< Let clients try to name the new style.

Preparation
%< **Two Months Before:** Place an ad in newspaper and get copy of the ad slick to use for flyers. (Buy neon paper to run flyers on.)

%< **One Month Before:** Distribute flyers as bag stuffers. Notify current clients by posting a flyer on your bulletin board for a month previous to the promotion and mailing one to clients who have not been in for 3 months.

Meet with salon staff and explain the promo to everyone. Give all a stack of flyers to distribute.

%< **One Week Before:** Double check with the newspaper.

%< **One Day Before the Ad Runs:** Review promo with staff. Make copy of the tracking sheet.

Estimated Cost
%< $20-30 if only flyers used. Additional cost for newspaper ad—depends on ad size and newspaper rates. Also, remember to allocate additional money for postage if flyer is mailed out.

PROMOTION TRACKING SHEET

(Keep This on a Clipboard at the Reception Desk)

NAME OF PROMOTION

DATE PROMO STARTS   DATE PROMO ENDS

AMOUNT OF NEW CUSTOMERS

	SUN	MON	TUE	WED	THU	FRI	SAT
Week 1							
Week 2							
Week 3							
Week 4							
Monthly Total							

(At the end of every day, take a moment to jot down the number of clients this promotion brought in. At the end of the promotion, total all of the weekly results for a grand total of client responses to this promotion. Be sure to note bad weather, illness, or any mishaps that may have interfered with your promotion's potential success.)

RETRO HAIRSTYLE PHOTO CONTEST

Bring us in a photo of you
in a style that matches a

Popular Movie Star From The 60'S

Show us your 60's Beehive or Flip

SALON NAME
ADDRESS
PHONE

Customers May Enter Contest at Point of Purchase

RETRO HAIRSTYLE PHOTO CONTEST PROMOTION

Objective

✂ Reach new clients. Have a blast from the past with old clients

Description

✂ All customers who purchase any service can enter the photo contest —they just bring in a photo of themselves in a high fashion, movie star style from the 1960's.

Preparation

✂ Meet with salon staff and explain the promo to everyone. Make a poster to announce the contest. Make a display board for photos. Make copy of the tracking sheet.

Estimated Cost

✂ $2 for poster board

PROMOTION TRACKING SHEET

(Keep This on a Clipboard at the Reception Desk)

_____

NAME OF PROMOTION

_____   _____

DATE PROMO STARTS   DATE PROMO ENDS

_____

AMOUNT OF NEW CUSTOMERS

	SUN	MON	TUE	WED	THU	FRI	SAT
Week 1							
Week 2							
Week 3							
Week 4							
Monthly Total							

(At the end of every day, take a moment to jot down the number of clients this promotion brought in. At the end of the promotion, total all of the weekly results for a grand total of client responses to this promotion. Be sure to note bad weather, illness, or any mishaps that may have interfered with your promotion's potential success.)

A PRIVATE ISSUE

SALON NAME
Address
Phone

Many women have thinning hair, but they don't have to look like it. Try on our state of the art wiglets and see yourself in fuller, bouncier hair.

Invites you to experience our private issue wiglet show.

We will show you our exclusive line of human hair wiglets in the privacy of a closed booth.

Don't let thinning hair affect your lifestyle, let us show you how a wiglet can help you have thicker, fuller hair.

Call for your appointment today
Consultations are free

PRIVATE ISSUE PROMOTION

Objective
✂ Introduce clients with thinning hair to the benefits of a wiglet.

Description
✂ Offer a free consultation to clients with thinning hair.

Preparation
✂ Meet with salon staff and explain the promo to everyone. Be sure all are trained in wiglet care.

Send out notes to clients as you notice the need for a wiglet, or as clients are referred to you.

Estimated Cost
✂ $20–30 if only flyers used, additional cost for postage. Be sure to stock a full line of wiglets.

PROMOTION TRACKING SHEET

(Keep This on a Clipboard at the Reception Desk)

_____

NAME OF PROMOTION

_____   _____

DATE PROMO STARTS   DATE PROMO ENDS

_____

AMOUNT OF NEW CUSTOMERS

	SUN	MON	TUE	WED	THU	FRI	SAT
Week 1							
Week 2							
Week 3							
Week 4							
Monthly Total							

(At the end of every day, take a moment to jot down the number of clients this promotion brought in. At the end of the promotion, total all of the weekly results for a grand total of client responses to this promotion. Be sure to note bad weather, illness, or any mishaps that may have interfered with your promotion's potential success.)

TREATMENTS FOR THINNING HAIR

Gentlemen,

Let us help you keep the

hair you have years longer.

Attend our healthy hair

and scalp workshop.

Date__ / __ / __

FREE WORKSHOP—MONDAYS AT 7 PM.

LEARN HOW TO PROPERLY SHAMPOO, CONDITION,

AND CARE FOR YOUR SCALP AND HAIR.

Salon Name
Address
Phone

Call for an Appointment Today

HOW TO GET YOUR MAN—THIN HAIR PROMOTION

Objective
✂ Reach new clients and help current ones, too.

Description
✂ Offer a free consultation and hair and scalp classes.

Preparation
✂ Meet with salon staff and explain the promo to everyone.

Duplicate and send out letters to every client with thin hair. Place a letter in every retail bag.

Estimated Cost
✂ $20–30 if only letters used. Additional cost for postage if mailed.

PROMOTION TRACKING SHEET

(Keep This on a Clipboard at the Reception Desk)

_____

NAME OF PROMOTION

_____   _____

DATE PROMO STARTS   DATE PROMO ENDS

_____

AMOUNT OF NEW CUSTOMERS

	SUN	MON	TUE	WED	THU	FRI	SAT
Week 1							
Week 2							
Week 3							
Week 4							
Monthly Total							

(At the end of every day, take a moment to jot down the number of clients this promotion brought in. At the end of the promotion, total all of the weekly results for a grand total of client responses to this promotion. Be sure to note bad weather, illness, or any mishaps that may have interfered with your promotion's potential success.)

Baby's First Haircut

SALON NAME
ADDRESS
PHONE

IS PLEASED TO OFFER
YOUR BABY
IT'S FIRST HAIRCUT IN A
SPECIAL WAY!!

WE WILL PRESERVE THE MEMORY FOR ETERNITY.
WE WILL TAKE A PHOTO OF THE BIG EVENT AND ATTACH A LOCK
OF HAIR TO THE PHOTO.

AS ALWAYS, CHILDREN'S CUTS ARE ONLY $1 PER YEAR OLD

BABY'S FIRST HAIRCUT PROMOTION

Objective

✄Reach new clients through baby's cuts.

Description

✄Offer a free photo of the big day and a special price.

Preparation

✄**Two Months Before**: Place an ad in newspaper. Get copy of the ad slick to use for flyers. (Buy neon paper to run flyers on.)

Stock several boxes of instant film.

✄**One Month Before**: Distribute flyers as bag stuffers (baby stores, nursery schools, welcome wagon). Notify current clients by posting a flyer on your bulletin board for a month previous to the promotion.

Meet with salon staff and explain the promo to everyone. Give all a stack of flyers to distribute.

✄**One Week Before**: Double check with the newspaper, be sure you have enough film. Post lots of baby photos in salon.

✄**One Day Before the Ad Runs**: Review promo with staff. Make copy of the tracking sheet.

Estimated Cost

✄$20-30 if only flyers used. Additional cost for newspaper ad—depends on ad size and newspaper rates. Also, remember to allocate additional money for film.

PROMOTION TRACKING SHEET

(Keep This on a Clipboard at the Reception Desk)

_____

NAME OF PROMOTION

_____   _____

DATE PROMO STARTS   DATE PROMO ENDS

_____

AMOUNT OF NEW CUSTOMERS

	SUN	MON	TUE	WED	THU	FRI	SAT
Week 1							
Week 2							
Week 3							
Week 4							
Monthly Total							

(At the end of every day, take a moment to jot down the number of clients this promotion brought in. At the end of the promotion, total all of the weekly results for a grand total of client responses to this promotion. Be sure to note bad weather, illness, or any mishaps that may have interfered with your promotion's potential success.)

SPRING LIFE INTO YOUR HAIR

Spring is the
perfect time to
have a growth
stimulation and
scalp treatment.

✤

Try our new
"Natural Fragrance"
treatments, 20% off all
treatments in March.

✤

Healthy scalps
encourage hair growth

✤

Salon Name
Address
Phone

Selected Stylists Only

SPRING—HAIR TREATMENT PROMOTION

Objective
✄Reach new clients. Help current clients have healthier hair.

Description
✄Offer a discount for a treatment during spring.

Preparation
✄**Two Months Before:** Place an ad in newspaper and get copy of the ad slick to use for flyers. (Buy neon paper to run flyers on.)

Stock several cases of treatments. Check for co-op money with manufacturers. The company that made the treatment may offer rebates to help you with the promo cost.

✄**One Month Before:** Distribute flyers as bag stuffers (department stores, resorts, beach hotels, schools). Notify current clients by posting a flyer on your bulletin board for a month previous to the promotion.

Meet with salon staff and explain the promo to everyone. Give all a stack of flyers to distribute.

✄**One Week Before:** Double check with the newspaper, be sure you have enough product. Display it in salon.

✄**One Day Before the Ad Runs:** Review promo with staff. Make copy of the tracking sheet.

Estimated Cost
✄$20-30 if only flyers used. Additional cost for newspaper ad—depends on ad size and newspaper rates.

PROMOTION TRACKING SHEET

(Keep This on a Clipboard at the Reception Desk)

_____

NAME OF PROMOTION

_____   _____

DATE PROMO STARTS   DATE PROMO ENDS

_____

AMOUNT OF NEW CUSTOMERS

	SUN	MON	TUE	WED	THU	FRI	SAT
Week 1							
Week 2							
Week 3							
Week 4							
Monthly Total							

(At the end of every day, take a moment to jot down the number of clients this promotion brought in. At the end of the promotion, total all of the weekly results for a grand total of client responses to this promotion. Be sure to note bad weather, illness, or any mishaps that may have interfered with your promotion's potential success.)

A FAMILY AFFAIR

During the month of May, families enjoy 50% off haircuts when you book your appointments together!

A sure fire winner! 50% off 2 or more cuts for family members.

Salon Name
Address
Phone

CALL FOR YOUR APPOINTMENT TODAY

SELECTED STYLISTS ONLY

FAMILY AFFAIR DISCOUNT PROMOTION

Objective

ℰ< Reach new family members and new clients.

Description

ℰ< Offer a discount when two or more family members have their hair done, together.

Preparation

ℰ< **Two Months Before:** Place an ad in newspaper and get copy of the ad slick to use for flyers. (Buy neon paper to run flyers on.)

ℰ< **One Month Before:** Distribute flyers as bag stuffers (stores, resorts, hotels, schools). Notify current clients by posting a flyer on your bulletin board for a month previous to the promotion.

Meet with salon staff and explain the promo to everyone. Give all a stack of flyers to distribute.

ℰ< **One Week Before:** Double check with the newspaper.

ℰ< **One Day Before the Ad Runs:** Review promo with staff. Make copy of the tracking sheet.

Estimated Cost

ℰ< $20-30 if only flyers used. Additional cost for newspaper ad—depends on ad size and newspaper rates.

PROMOTION TRACKING SHEET

(Keep This on a Clipboard at the Reception Desk)

_____

NAME OF PROMOTION

_____   _____

DATE PROMO STARTS   DATE PROMO ENDS

_____

AMOUNT OF NEW CUSTOMERS

	SUN	MON	TUE	WED	THU	FRI	SAT
Week 1							
Week 2							
Week 3							
Week 4							
Monthly Total							

(At the end of every day, take a moment to jot down the number of clients this promotion brought in. At the end of the promotion, total all of the weekly results for a grand total of client responses to this promotion. Be sure to note bad weather, illness, or any mishaps that may have interfered with your promotion's potential success.)

COLOR YOU CHANGED PROMOTION

Objective
✄ Reach new color clients.

Description
✄ Offer a $10 off coupon for all color services.

Preparation
✄ **Two Months Before**: Place an ad in newspaper and get copy of the ad slick to use for flyers. (Buy neon paper to run flyers on.)

Stock extra color. Check for co-op money with color manufacturers. (The company that made the color may offer rebates to help you with the promo cost.)

✄ **One Month Before**: Distribute flyers as bag stuffers (stores, resorts, hotels, schools). Notify current clients by posting a flyer on your bulletin board for a month previous to the promotion.

Meet with salon staff and explain the promo to everyone. Give all a stack of flyers to distribute.

✄ **One Week Before**: Double check with the newspaper, be sure you have enough color, set up a display in salon.

✄ **One Day Before the Ad Runs**: Review promo with staff. Make copy of the tracking sheet.

Estimated Cost
✄ $20-30 if only flyers used. Additional cost for newspaper ad—depends on ad size and newspaper rates. Also, remember to allocate additional supply $ for extra color needed.

PROMOTION
TRACKING SHEET

(Keep This on a Clipboard at the Reception Desk)

_____

NAME OF PROMOTION

_____   _____

DATE PROMO STARTS   DATE PROMO ENDS

_____

AMOUNT OF NEW CUSTOMERS

	SUN	MON	TUE	WED	THU	FRI	SAT
Week 1							
Week 2							
Week 3							
Week 4							
Monthly Total							

(At the end of every day, take a moment to jot down the number of clients this promotion brought in. At the end of the promotion, total all of the weekly results for a grand total of client responses to this promotion. Be sure to note bad weather, illness, or any mishaps that may have interfered with your promotion's potential success.)

Believe it or Not, You Just Found A Dollar

As a valued male client, we would like to invite you to save a buck all year long! Just bring in this Salon Dollar and save!

ONE SALON DOLLAR

ONE SALON DOLLAR

USE THIS DOLLAR ON EVERY HAIRCUT ALL YEAR LONG

Salon Name
Address & Phone

Happy Independence Day!

Expires 12/31/97

MAIL TO MALES PROMOTION

Objective
✄ Encourage new and repeat cuts for male clients.

Description
✄ Offer a $1 off all haircuts this July–December.

Preparation
✄ **One Month Before:** Mail flyers to all male clients. Notify current clients by posting a flyer on your bulletin board for a month previous to the promotion.

Meet with salon staff and explain the promo to everyone. Give all a stack of flyers to distribute.

Estimated Cost
✄ $20–30 if only flyers used. Additional cost for postage.

(Note: This flyer can be changed to suit any holiday.)

PROMOTION TRACKING SHEET

(Keep This on a Clipboard at the Reception Desk)

_____

NAME OF PROMOTION

_____   _____

DATE PROMO STARTS   DATE PROMO ENDS

_____

AMOUNT OF NEW CUSTOMERS

	SUN	MON	TUE	WED	THU	FRI	SAT
Week 1							
Week 2							
Week 3							
Week 4							
Monthly Total							

(At the end of every day, take a moment to jot down the number of clients this promotion brought in. At the end of the promotion, total all of the weekly results for a grand total of client responses to this promotion. Be sure to note bad weather, illness, or any mishaps that may have interfered with your promotion's potential success.)

HAPPY BIRTHDAY!

Enjoy This Gift:
A _FREE_ Manicure
With Your Next
Regular Haircut Appointment

Happy Birthday to our treasured client. Mention this coupon when you book your next appointment! We will treat you to a _FREE MANICURE!_

SALON NAME
Phone
Address

MANY HAPPY RETURNS!!

BIRTHDAY CARD COUPON PROMOTION

Objective
✂ Reward existing clients.

Description
✂ Offer a free manicure with any appointment.

Preparation
✂ **Every Month**: Check client record cards and send out flyers. Meet with salon staff and explain the promo to everyone.

Estimated Cost
✂ $20–30 if only flyers used. Additional cost for postage.

PROMOTION TRACKING SHEET

(Keep This on a Clipboard at the Reception Desk)

_____

NAME OF PROMOTION

_____   _____

DATE PROMO STARTS   DATE PROMO ENDS

_____

AMOUNT OF NEW CUSTOMERS

	SUN	MON	TUE	WED	THU	FRI	SAT
Week 1							
Week 2							
Week 3							
Week 4							
Monthly Total							

(At the end of every day, take a moment to jot down the number of clients this promotion brought in. At the end of the promotion, total all of the weekly results for a grand total of client responses to this promotion. Be sure to note bad weather, illness, or any mishaps that may have interfered with your promotion's potential success.)

Guess What's Missing?

You Are!

Stop in and see what's new and exciting this fall. We even have a gift for you.

You Ought to See What You've Been Missing

We Miss You!

Salon Name

Address

Phone

GUESS WHAT'S MISSING PROMOTION

Objective
✂ Reach professional clients who haven't been in lately.

Description
✂ Offer a free gift (nail file or shampoo sample).

Preparation
✂ Create your own flyer. Mail them to clients. Stock several give away gifts.

Meet with salon staff and explain the promo to everyone. Give all a stack of flyers to use.

Estimated Cost
✂ $20–30 if only flyers used. Additional cost for postage.

PROMOTION TRACKING SHEET

(Keep This on a Clipboard at the Reception Desk)

_____

NAME OF PROMOTION

_____   _____

DATE PROMO STARTS   DATE PROMO ENDS

_____

AMOUNT OF NEW CUSTOMERS

	SUN	MON	TUE	WED	THU	FRI	SAT
Week 1							
Week 2							
Week 3							
Week 4							
Monthly Total							

(At the end of every day, take a moment to jot down the number of clients this promotion brought in. At the end of the promotion, total all of the weekly results for a grand total of client responses to this promotion. Be sure to note bad weather, illness, or any mishaps that may have interfered with your promotion's potential success.)

ONE DAY PERM SALE

Salon Name

Is Proud to Offer You

Our $100 Perm for *Only $50*

Glorious curls, perms at half-price

•

Stop in or call on Monday, June 15, to purchase a certificate for a perm, which can be used any Monday, Tuesday or Wednesday in 1998. With selected stylists.

•

Certificates must be purchased on July 15 to receive the half-price offer.
All certificates must be paid in full on the 15th of June.

•

Cash, checks, credit cards accepted. Phone orders taken with credit cards.

•

Offer limited to three coupons per client.

Phone Number • Fax Number

$100 Perm Certificate $100 Perm Certificate

SALON NAME

Authorized Signature

Expiration Date

Valid

$100 Perm Certificate $100 Perm Certificate

ONE DAY PERM SALE PROMOTION

Objective
✂ Reach new perm clients.

Description
✂ Offer a half-price perm if paid for in advance.

Preparation
✂ **Two Months Before:** Place an ad in newspaper and get copy of the ad slick to use for flyers. (Buy neon paper to run flyers on.) Send flyers to clients. Make copies of a certificate to sell.

Check for co-op money with perm manufacturers. (The company that made the perms may offer rebates to help you with the promo cost.)

✂ **One Month Before:** Meet with salon staff and explain the promo to everyone. Give all a stack of flyers to distribute.

✂ **One Week Before:** Double check with the newspaper, be sure you have enough coupons, display one!

✂ **One Day Before the Ad Runs:** Review promo with staff. Make copy of the tracking sheet.

Estimated Cost
✂ Newspaper ad—depends on ad size and newspaper rates. Also, remember to print coupons.

PROMOTION
TRACKING SHEET

(Keep This on a Clipboard at the Reception Desk)

_____
NAME OF PROMOTION

_____   _____
DATE PROMO STARTS   DATE PROMO ENDS

_____
AMOUNT OF NEW CUSTOMERS

	SUN	MON	TUE	WED	THU	FRI	SAT
Week 1							
Week 2							
Week 3							
Week 4							
Monthly Total							

(At the end of every day, take a moment to jot down the number of clients this promotion brought in. At the end of the promotion, total all of the weekly results for a grand total of client responses to this promotion. Be sure to note bad weather, illness, or any mishaps that may have interfered with your promotion's potential success.)

HAIRCUT CARD

GET YOUR CARD SIGNED EVERY TIME YOU
GET A HAIRCUT AND
The 10th One Is **FREE**

DATE:

SIGNATURE:

DATE:

SIGNATURE:

DATE:

SIGNATURE:

DATE:

SIGNATURE:

DATE:

SIGNATURE

DATE:

SIGNATURE:

DATE:

SIGNATURE:

DATE:

SIGNATURE:

DATE:

SIGNATURE:

DATE: **TENTH CUT IS FREE!**

SALON NAME
Address
PHONE

CUT CARDS PROMOTION

Objective
✂ Reach new haircut clients.

Description
✂ Offer a free haircut with the purchase of nine cuts.

Preparation
✂ Have cards printed and give them out to all clients.

Meet with salon staff and explain the promo to everyone. Give all a stack of flyers to distribute.

Estimated Cost
✂ $20–30 for cards to be printed.

PROMOTION TRACKING SHEET

(Keep This on a Clipboard at the Reception Desk)

_____

NAME OF PROMOTION

_____   _____

DATE PROMO STARTS   DATE PROMO ENDS

_____

AMOUNT OF NEW CUSTOMERS

	SUN	MON	TUE	WED	THU	FRI	SAT
Week 1							
Week 2							
Week 3							
Week 4							
Monthly Total							

(At the end of every day, take a moment to jot down the number of clients this promotion brought in. At the end of the promotion, total all of the weekly results for a grand total of client responses to this promotion. Be sure to note bad weather, illness, or any mishaps that may have interfered with your promotion's potential success.)

Customer Appreciation Days June 3–10, 1997

SALON NAME

Is pleased to reward all our loyal customers with a party!

Receive A *FREE GIFT* and A 20% Discount on All Services with Selected Stylists

Refreshments Served
Fun for all!

Salon Name
Address
Phone

WE APPRECIATE YOU!

CUSTOMER APPRECIATION DAYS PROMOTION

Objective

✄ Reach clients not in for a while and reward steady clients for loyalty.

Description

✄ Offer a free gift, discount, and a party.

Preparation

✄ **One Month Before:** Distribute flyers as bag stuffers and through your mailing list. Notify current clients by posting a flyer on your bulletin board for a month previous to the promotion.

Meet with salon staff and explain the promo to everyone. Give all a stack of flyers to distribute.

✄ **One Day Before:** Review promo with staff. Make copy of the tracking sheet.

Estimated Cost

✄ $20–30 if only flyers used. Additional cost for gifts and postage. Keep refreshments simple.

PROMOTION TRACKING SHEET

(Keep This on a Clipboard at the Reception Desk)

_____

NAME OF PROMOTION

_____   _____

DATE PROMO STARTS   DATE PROMO ENDS

_____

AMOUNT OF NEW CUSTOMERS

	SUN	MON	TUE	WED	THU	FRI	SAT
Week 1							
Week 2							
Week 3							
Week 4							
Monthly Total							

(At the end of every day, take a moment to jot down the number of clients this promotion brought in. At the end of the promotion, total all of the weekly results for a grand total of client responses to this promotion. Be sure to note bad weather, illness, or any mishaps that may have interfered with your promotion's potential success.)

Let Us Fly You Away To A World Of Luxury

Facials Half-Price Today!

SALON NAME
Address
Phone

PROMO CARDS FOR THE MIRRORS PROMOTION

Objective
✄ Sell new services to current clients.

Description
✄ Offer a half price service by placing a card or flyer on each mirror in the salon. This is a great way to introduce a new stylist, service or to beef up tickets from repeat clients.

Meet with salon staff and explain the promo to everyone. Give all a card to put on their mirror on designated days.

Make copy of the tracking sheet.

Estimated Cost
✄ $20–30 if only flyers used.

PROMOTION TRACKING SHEET

(Keep This on a Clipboard at the Reception Desk)

_____

NAME OF PROMOTION

_____   _____

DATE PROMO STARTS   DATE PROMO ENDS

_____

AMOUNT OF NEW CUSTOMERS

	SUN	MON	TUE	WED	THU	FRI	SAT
Week 1							
Week 2							
Week 3							
Week 4							
Monthly Total							

(At the end of every day, take a moment to jot down the number of clients this promotion brought in. At the end of the promotion, total all of the weekly results for a grand total of client responses to this promotion. Be sure to note bad weather, illness, or any mishaps that may have interfered with your promotion's potential success.)

HERE COMES THE BRIDE—MANICURE PROMOTION

Objective
✂ Reach new clients.

Description
✂ Offer a free manicure on a bride's wedding day, if she has her hair done in your salon.

Preparation
✂ **Two Months Before**: Create flyers. Distribute flyers as bag stuffers (bridal stores and photographers). Notify current clients by posting a flyer on your bulletin board for a month previous to the promotion.

Meet with salon staff and explain the promo to everyone. Give all a stack of flyers to distribute.

✂ **One Day Before**: Review promo with staff. Make copy of the tracking sheet.

Estimated Cost
✂ $20–30 if only flyers used.

PROMOTION
TRACKING SHEET

(Keep This on a Clipboard at the Reception Desk)

_____

NAME OF PROMOTION

_____   _____

DATE PROMO STARTS   DATE PROMO ENDS

_____

AMOUNT OF NEW CUSTOMERS

	SUN	MON	TUE	WED	THU	FRI	SAT
Week 1							
Week 2							
Week 3							
Week 4							
Monthly Total							

(At the end of every day, take a moment to jot down the number of clients this promotion brought in. At the end of the promotion, total all of the weekly results for a grand total of client responses to this promotion. Be sure to note bad weather, illness, or any mishaps that may have interfered with your promotion's potential success.)

WANTED:

*(place a photo of
a messy haired person here)*

DEAD OR ALIVE
(Preferably Alive)

Refer 2 of your friends to us and
receive a *FREE* haircut!

Offer Expires 1/23/98

WANTED DEAD OR ALIVE PROMOTION

Objective
✄ Reach new clients.

Description
✄ Offer current clients a free haircut in return for 2 referrals.

Preparation
✄ Create a flyer. (Insert your special photo, too! Use staff photos.) Meet with salon staff and explain the promo to everyone. Give all a stack of flyers to distribute. Make copy of tracking sheet. Pass out flyers in salon and mail to client list.

Estimated Cost
✄ $20–30 if only flyers used.

PROMOTION TRACKING SHEET

(Keep This on a Clipboard at the Reception Desk)

_____

NAME OF PROMOTION

_____   _____

DATE PROMO STARTS   DATE PROMO ENDS

_____

AMOUNT OF NEW CUSTOMERS

	SUN	MON	TUE	WED	THU	FRI	SAT
Week 1							
Week 2							
Week 3							
Week 4							
Monthly Total							

(At the end of every day, take a moment to jot down the number of clients this promotion brought in. At the end of the promotion, total all of the weekly results for a grand total of client responses to this promotion. Be sure to note bad weather, illness, or any mishaps that may have interfered with your promotion's potential success.)

SALUTE TO PARIS PROMOTION

Objective
✄ Reach new manicure clients.

Preparation
✄ **Two Months Before:** Place an ad in newspaper and get copy of the ad slick to use for flyers. (Buy neon paper to run flyers on.)

✄ **One Month Before:** Distribute flyers as bag stuffers (dress shops, stores, resorts, hotels, schools). Notify current clients by posting a flyer on your bulletin board for a month previous to the promotion.

Meet with salon staff and explain the promo to everyone. Give all a stack of flyers to distribute.

✄ **One Week Before:** Double check with the newspaper, be sure you have enough polish and display it in salon.

✄ **One Day Before the Ad Runs:** Review promo with staff. Make copy of the tracking sheet.

Estimated Cost
✄ $20–30 if only flyers used. Additional cost for newspaper ad—depends on ad size and newspaper rates.

PROMOTION
TRACKING SHEET

(Keep This on a Clipboard at the Reception Desk)

_____

NAME OF PROMOTION

_____   _____

DATE PROMO STARTS   DATE PROMO ENDS

_____

AMOUNT OF NEW CUSTOMERS

	SUN	MON	TUE	WED	THU	FRI	SAT
Week 1							
Week 2							
Week 3							
Week 4							
Monthly Total							

(At the end of every day, take a moment to jot down the number of clients this promotion brought in. At the end of the promotion, total all of the weekly results for a grand total of client responses to this promotion. Be sure to note bad weather, illness, or any mishaps that may have interfered with your promotion's potential success.)

AN INVE$TMENT IN YOUR APPEARANCE

Invest one afternoon with us
and let us pamper you!

Start with a hairstyle,
next add a manicure and
have a pedicure, too.

$10 OFF ALL THREE SERVICES

SALON NAME
Address
Phone

Feel like a million bucks!

AN INVESTMENT IN YOUR APPEARANCE PROMOTION

Objective

✂ Reach new clients .

Description

✂ Mail this flyer to every branch of local banks.

Preparation

✂ Meet with salon staff and explain the promo to everyone. Give all a stack of flyers to distribute.

Make copy of the tracking sheet.

Estimated Cost

✂ $20–30 if only flyers used and budget for postage.

PROMOTION TRACKING SHEET

(Keep This on a Clipboard at the Reception Desk)

_____

NAME OF PROMOTION

_____   _____

DATE PROMO STARTS   DATE PROMO ENDS

_____

AMOUNT OF NEW CUSTOMERS

	SUN	MON	TUE	WED	THU	FRI	SAT
Week 1							
Week 2							
Week 3							
Week 4							
Monthly Total							

(At the end of every day, take a moment to jot down the number of clients this promotion brought in. At the end of the promotion, total all of the weekly results for a grand total of client responses to this promotion. Be sure to note bad weather, illness, or any mishaps that may have interfered with your promotion's potential success.)

AFTERNOON DELIGHT PROMOTION

Objective
✄ Fill in for canceled appointments on rainy afternoons.

Description
✄ Offer a free ice cream treat while client is under your dryer.

Preparation
✄ Create your salon's flyer.

Make an agreement with an ice cream shop in the area, or learn to make sundaes!

✄ **One Month Before:** Distribute flyers as bag stuffers (stores, resorts, offices, and, schools). Notify current clients by posting a flyer on your bulletin board for a month previous to the promotion.

Meet with salon staff and explain the promo to everyone. Give all a stack of flyers to distribute.

Make copy of the tracking sheet.

Estimated Cost
✄ $20–30 if only flyers used. Additional cost for ice cream sundaes.

PROMOTION TRACKING SHEET

(Keep This on a Clipboard at the Reception Desk)

_____

NAME OF PROMOTION

_____   _____

DATE PROMO STARTS   DATE PROMO ENDS

_____

AMOUNT OF NEW CUSTOMERS

	SUN	MON	TUE	WED	THU	FRI	SAT
Week 1							
Week 2							
Week 3							
Week 4							
Monthly Total							

(At the end of every day, take a moment to jot down the number of clients this promotion brought in. At the end of the promotion, total all of the weekly results for a grand total of client responses to this promotion. Be sure to note bad weather, illness, or any mishaps that may have interfered with your promotion's potential success.)

We want to help you put your best foot forward

1
2

Price Pedicure

with the Purchase

of Sandals.

Dance into our salon…

Where you are

always first!

Salon Name

Address

Phone

Selected Manicurists

(The above salon will honor this coupon for a half-price manicure.)

SHOE BIZ PROMOTION

Objective

✄ Reach new clients.

Description

✄ Offer a free or a discounted pedicure, by giving a local shoe store one of these certificates—flyers to give to every client who buys sandals this month. You can even offer to stuff the boxes of sandals yourself!! The shoe store may want to put sale flyers in your salon, in exchange for helping you.

Preparation

✄ **Two Months Before:** Buy neon paper to run flyers on. Use the promo to create your own flyers. Talk to a few shoe stores to find one that is interested in the promotion. Distribute flyers as bag stuffers. Meet with salon staff and explain the promo to everyone. Make copy of the tracking sheet.

Estimated Cost

✄ $20–30 if only flyers used.

Note: This promo works with hats (haircuts), rings (manicures), earrings (facials or make-overs), and swimsuits (waxing).

PROMOTION TRACKING SHEET

(Keep This on a Clipboard at the Reception Desk)

_____

NAME OF PROMOTION

_____   _____

DATE PROMO STARTS   DATE PROMO ENDS

_____

AMOUNT OF NEW CUSTOMERS

	SUN	MON	TUE	WED	THU	FRI	SAT
Week 1							
Week 2							
Week 3							
Week 4							
Monthly Total							

(At the end of every day, take a moment to jot down the number of clients this promotion brought in. At the end of the promotion, total all of the weekly results for a grand total of client responses to this promotion. Be sure to note bad weather, illness, or any mishaps that may have interfered with your promotion's potential success.)

Have Lunch
At Our Place

We will have lunch delivered to you
while you enjoy a relaxing pedicure in
our new pedicure throne.

Salon Name
Phone

Lunch and pedicure **guaranteed**
in an hour!

LUNCH AT OUR PLACE PROMOTION

Objective

✂ Reach busy clients who do not have a lot of time.

Description

✂ Join forces with a local restaurant that delivers. Help clients kill two birds with one stone, lunch and a pampering service.

Preparation

✂ **Two Months Before:** Place an ad in newspaper and get copy of the ad slick to use for flyers. (Buy neon paper to run flyers on.)

Meet with restaurants and get their menus.

✂ **One Month Before:** Distribute flyers to offices and schools. Notify current clients by posting a flyer on your bulletin board for a month previous to the promotion.

Meet with salon staff and explain the promo to everyone. Give all a stack of flyers to distribute.

✂ **One Week Before:** Double check with the newspaper.

✂ **One Day Before the Ad Runs:** Review promo with staff. Make copy of the tracking sheet.

Estimated Cost

✂ $20-30 if only flyers used. Additional cost for newspaper ad—depends on ad size and newspaper rates. Food is added to client's bill, so there is no cost to salon.

PROMOTION TRACKING SHEET

(Keep This on a Clipboard at the Reception Desk)

_____
NAME OF PROMOTION

_____   _____
DATE PROMO STARTS   DATE PROMO ENDS

_____
AMOUNT OF NEW CUSTOMERS

	SUN	MON	TUE	WED	THU	FRI	SAT
Week 1							
Week 2							
Week 3							
Week 4							
Monthly Total							

(At the end of every day, take a moment to jot down the number of clients this promotion brought in. At the end of the promotion, total all of the weekly results for a grand total of client responses to this promotion. Be sure to note bad weather, illness, or any mishaps that may have interfered with your promotion's potential success.)

TEMPS DESERVE A BREAK!

SALON NAME
Address
Phone
Is pleased to offer
temps from the
(Agency Name)

A **_FREE_** Makeover

Let Us Help You
Fit the Corporate Image

Call for an appointment today!

TEMPS DESERVE A BREAK PROMOTION

Objective

✂ Reach new clients.

Description

✂ Offer a free make over for temporary employment agency workers.

Preparation

✂ Write a letter to the agency and attach a copy of your promo. Let the agency know you will be doing this gratis service on slow times, as you are able to meet with salon staff and explain the promo to everyone. Make copy of the tracking sheet.

Estimated Cost

✂ $20–30 if only flyers used.

PROMOTION TRACKING SHEET

(Keep This on a Clipboard at the Reception Desk)

_____

NAME OF PROMOTION

_____   _____

DATE PROMO STARTS   DATE PROMO ENDS

_____

AMOUNT OF NEW CUSTOMERS

	SUN	MON	TUE	WED	THU	FRI	SAT
Week 1							
Week 2							
Week 3							
Week 4							
Monthly Total							

(At the end of every day, take a moment to jot down the number of clients this promotion brought in. At the end of the promotion, total all of the weekly results for a grand total of client responses to this promotion. Be sure to note bad weather, illness, or any mishaps that may have interfered with your promotion's potential success.)

Beat The Blues

Salon Name
Address
Phone

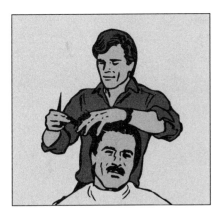

We offer police officers
special treatments and haircuts
to help you with
"hat hair"
(the marks that your hat makes on your hair)

Call for an appointment today!

BEAT THE BLUES PROMOTION

Objective
✂ Reach new haircut clients.

Description
✂ Send flyers to police academies, F.O.P clubs, etc. (F.O.P. means: fraternal order of police).

Preparation
✂ Meet with salon staff and explain the promo to everyone. Give all a stack of flyers to distribute. Make copy of the tracking sheet.

Estimated Cost
✂ $20–30 if only flyers used.

PROMOTION TRACKING SHEET

(Keep This on a Clipboard at the Reception Desk)

_____

NAME OF PROMOTION

_____   _____

DATE PROMO STARTS   DATE PROMO ENDS

_____

AMOUNT OF NEW CUSTOMERS

	SUN	MON	TUE	WED	THU	FRI	SAT
Week 1							
Week 2							
Week 3							
Week 4							
Monthly Total							

(At the end of every day, take a moment to jot down the number of clients this promotion brought in. At the end of the promotion, total all of the weekly results for a grand total of client responses to this promotion. Be sure to note bad weather, illness, or any mishaps that may have interfered with your promotion's potential success.)

Book Worm Club

All summer long
we will give kids
age 12 and under
a free book to read
while they get
their haircut.
(And they can take it
home with them!)

SALON NAME
Address
Phone

*Reading is a child's key
to success!*

BOOK WORM PROMOTION

Objective
✄Reach children as new haircut clients.

Description
✄Offer a free book with every haircut.

Preparation
✄**Two Months Before:** Shop flea markets, close-out sales, etc. Stock up on inexpensive kids' books. Make copies of this flyer and mail to clients. Notify current clients by posting a flyer on your bulletin board for a month previous to the promotion.

Meet with salon staff and explain the promo to everyone. Give all a stack of flyers to distribute.

Make copy of the tracking sheet.

Estimated Cost
✄$20-30 for flyers used. Additional cost for postage and books.

PROMOTION TRACKING SHEET

(Keep This on a Clipboard at the Reception Desk)

_____

NAME OF PROMOTION

_____   _____

DATE PROMO STARTS   DATE PROMO ENDS

_____

AMOUNT OF NEW CUSTOMERS

	SUN	MON	TUE	WED	THU	FRI	SAT
Week 1							
Week 2							
Week 3							
Week 4							
Monthly Total							

(At the end of every day, take a moment to jot down the number of clients this promotion brought in. At the end of the promotion, total all of the weekly results for a grand total of client responses to this promotion. Be sure to note bad weather, illness, or any mishaps that may have interfered with your promotion's potential success.)

SALON NAME

Invites

(Insert Sorority Name)

For a Night of Fun

We'll make popcorn, swap gossip
and try new hairstyles,
nailpolish and facials.
We will even videotape the night
for your sorority to keep.

Date:

Time:

Place:

BRING A FRIEND!

COLLEGE DORM OR SORORITY PROMOTION

Objective
✂ Reach new clients.

Description
✂ Offer a fun night of trying new things.

Preparation
✂ **Two Months Before:** Send a letter to the sorority (or dormitory) attach a copy of your flyer. Meet with salon staff and explain the promo to everyone. Give all a stack of flyers to distribute.

Make copy of the tracking sheet.

Estimated Cost
✂ $20–30 if only flyers used. Additional cost for videotape ($5) and popcorn ($5).

PROMOTION
TRACKING SHEET

(Keep This on a Clipboard at the Reception Desk)

_____

NAME OF PROMOTION

_____   _____

DATE PROMO STARTS   DATE PROMO ENDS

_____

AMOUNT OF NEW CUSTOMERS

	SUN	MON	TUE	WED	THU	FRI	SAT
Week 1							
Week 2							
Week 3							
Week 4							
Monthly Total							

(At the end of every day, take a moment to jot down the number of clients this promotion brought in. At the end of the promotion, total all of the weekly results for a grand total of client responses to this promotion. Be sure to note bad weather, illness, or any mishaps that may have interfered with your promotion's potential success.)

What's **HOT**

AND

What's **NOT**

SALON NAME

Hair Fashion Show

Date
Time
Address
Phone

Join us for a
FREE fashion show
of the latest hairstyles
for holiday parties.

World Class Styling
for a
World Class Look!

Call for a reservation
Seating is limited

WHAT'S HOT AND WHAT'S NOT FASHION SHOW PROMOTION

Objective
✄ Reach new clients.

Description
✄ Offer a free fashion show for any civic group.

Preparation
✄ **Two Months Before:** Make copies of your flyer and send it to a few civic groups (PTA, Ladies clubs, etc.).

Ask a local dress shop to help dress the models in exchange for free publicity.

Notify current clients by posting a flyer on your bulletin board for a month previous to the promotion.

Meet with salon staff and explain the promo to everyone.

Estimated Cost
✄ $20–30 if only flyers used. Additional cost for postage.

PROMOTION TRACKING SHEET

(Keep This on a Clipboard at the Reception Desk)

_____

NAME OF PROMOTION

_____   _____

DATE PROMO STARTS   DATE PROMO ENDS

_____

AMOUNT OF NEW CUSTOMERS

	SUN	MON	TUE	WED	THU	FRI	SAT
Week 1							
Week 2							
Week 3							
Week 4							
Monthly Total							

(At the end of every day, take a moment to jot down the number of clients this promotion brought in. At the end of the promotion, total all of the weekly results for a grand total of client responses to this promotion. Be sure to note bad weather, illness, or any mishaps that may have interfered with your promotion's potential success.)

Time Changes Your Skin And Hair

Learn to Like Your Hair Again

Let us show you how to revive the youthful shine it use to have!

Stop In for a *FREE* Seminar

Salon Name

Address
Date & Time

Call for a reservation, space is limited.

SENIORS SEMINARS PROMOTION

Objective
✀ Reach new clients.

Description
✀ Offer a free seminar for senior citizens.

Preparation
✀ Mail a letter and copies of your flyer to local senior centers.

Notify current clients by posting a flyer on your bulletin board for a month previous to the promotion. Invite a clothing store to participate.

Meet with salon staff and explain the promo to everyone. Give all a stack of flyers to distribute.

Make copy of the tracking sheet.

Estimated Cost
✀ $20–30 if only flyers used. Additional cost for postage.

PROMOTION
TRACKING SHEET

(Keep This on a Clipboard at the Reception Desk)

_____

NAME OF PROMOTION

_____   _____

DATE PROMO STARTS   DATE PROMO ENDS

_____

AMOUNT OF NEW CUSTOMERS

	SUN	MON	TUE	WED	THU	FRI	SAT
Week 1							
Week 2							
Week 3							
Week 4							
Monthly Total							

(At the end of every day, take a moment to jot down the number of clients this promotion brought in. At the end of the promotion, total all of the weekly results for a grand total of client responses to this promotion. Be sure to note bad weather, illness, or any mishaps that may have interfered with your promotion's potential success.)

Salon Name

ADDRESS
PHONE

INVITES YOUR GRANDDAUGHTER
FOR A *FREE* MANICURE

BECAUSE YOU HAVE
BEEN SUCH A LOYAL CLIENT,
WE WOULD LIKE TO TREAT
YOUR SPECIAL GAL TO HER
FIRST SALON MANICURE, ON HER
NEXT BIRTHDAY!

*GIRLS AGE 4 AND UP
MAY PARTICIPATE.*

GRANDDAUGHTER'S FIRST MANICURE PROMOTION

Objective
✂ Reach clients.

Description
✂ Offer a free first manicure to your clients grandchild.

Preparation
✂ Create your flyer and mail it to your client list.

Post one on the salon bulletin board for a month previous to the promotion.

Meet with salon staff and explain the promo to everyone. Give all a stack of flyers to distribute.

Estimated Cost
✂ $20-30 if only flyers used. Additional cost for postage.

PROMOTION TRACKING SHEET

(Keep This on a Clipboard at the Reception Desk)

_____

NAME OF PROMOTION

_____ _____

DATE PROMO STARTS   DATE PROMO ENDS

_____

AMOUNT OF NEW CUSTOMERS

	SUN	MON	TUE	WED	THU	FRI	SAT
Week 1							
Week 2							
Week 3							
Week 4							
Monthly Total							

(At the end of every day, take a moment to jot down the number of clients this promotion brought in. At the end of the promotion, total all of the weekly results for a grand total of client responses to this promotion. Be sure to note bad weather, illness, or any mishaps that may have interfered with your promotion's potential success.)

★ SALON NAME ★

ADDRESS
PHONE

**Invites All Cast Members
Of The Community Theater
To Take**

A WHOPPING 50% OFF A PERM

**We will help you get your new look
ready for the stage.**

**Appointments Only
Selected Stylists**

COMMUNITY THEATER PROMOTION

Objective
✀ Reach new clients.

Description
✀ Offer a discount to cast members.

Preparation
✀ Create your flyer and mail it to local theater groups.

Post one on the salon bulletin board for a month previous to the promotion.

Meet with salon staff and explain the promo to everyone. Give all a stack of flyers to distribute.

Estimated Cost
✀ $20-30 if only flyers used. Additional cost for postage.

PROMOTION
TRACKING SHEET

(Keep This on a Clipboard at the Reception Desk)

_____
NAME OF PROMOTION

_____   _____
DATE PROMO STARTS   DATE PROMO ENDS

_____
AMOUNT OF NEW CUSTOMERS

	SUN	MON	TUE	WED	THU	FRI	SAT
Week 1							
Week 2							
Week 3							
Week 4							
Monthly Total							

(At the end of every day, take a moment to jot down the number of clients this promotion brought in. At the end of the promotion, total all of the weekly results for a grand total of client responses to this promotion. Be sure to note bad weather, illness, or any mishaps that may have interfered with your promotion's potential success.)

SALON NAME

ADDRESS
Phone
invites

Channel___ Anchor Team
For a **FREE** Makeover

FREE Makeovers
for all
Anchor Team Members

We want to update
your spring look
with
state of the art
styling and hair care

Great News
For Your News Team!

ANCHOR TEAM PROMOTION

Objective

- Reach new clients.

Description

- Offer a free makeover to anchor teams at local TV stations in exchange for a credit at the end of the program.

Preparation

- Write a letter to the station manager and make the offer to do free makeovers on the anchors.

Meet with salon staff and explain the promo to everyone. Give all a stack of flyers to distribute.

- *One Week Before the Makeovers:* Do a press release to all newspapers in the area. Review promo with staff.

Estimated Cost

- $.32 for postage, per letter and press release.

PROMOTION TRACKING SHEET

(Keep This on a Clipboard at the Reception Desk)

NAME OF PROMOTION

DATE PROMO STARTS   DATE PROMO ENDS

AMOUNT OF NEW CUSTOMERS

	SUN	MON	TUE	WED	THU	FRI	SAT
Week 1							
Week 2							
Week 3							
Week 4							
Monthly Total							

(At the end of every day, take a moment to jot down the number of clients this promotion brought in. At the end of the promotion, total all of the weekly results for a grand total of client responses to this promotion. Be sure to note bad weather, illness, or any mishaps that may have interfered with your promotion's potential success.)

Healthy Bodies Deserve Healthy Hair

This Month Only

Salon Name
Phone

Offers all health club members
20% Off All Services!

Pump some volume into your hair...
Let us build body into your tresses
Watch us construct a winning look

Healthy Hair and a Healthy Body
Go Hand in Hand!

HEALTHY HAIR PROMOTION

Objective
✂Reach new clients.

Description
✂Offer a discount to all health club members.

Preparation
✂**One Month Before:** Distribute flyers as mailers to all health clubs (don't forget the YWCA and YMCA).

Notify current clients by posting a flyer on your bulletin board for a month previous to the promotion.

Meet with salon staff and explain the promo to everyone. Give all a stack of flyers to distribute.

✂**One Day Before:** Review promo with staff. Make copy of the tracking sheet.

Estimated Cost
✂$.32 for postage, per health spa letter.

PROMOTION
TRACKING SHEET

(Keep This on a Clipboard at the Reception Desk)

_____

NAME OF PROMOTION

_____

DATE PROMO STARTS   DATE PROMO ENDS

_____

AMOUNT OF NEW CUSTOMERS

	SUN	MON	TUE	WED	THU	FRI	SAT
Week 1							
Week 2							
Week 3							
Week 4							
Monthly Total							

(At the end of every day, take a moment to jot down the number of clients this promotion brought in. At the end of the promotion, total all of the weekly results for a grand total of client responses to this promotion. Be sure to note bad weather, illness, or any mishaps that may have interfered with your promotion's potential success.)

Father and Son Haircut Day

Salon Name
Phone

Dedicates this Saturday as
**Father and Son
Haircut Day**

Check it out! Both have haircuts
but you only pay for one!

GREAT SAVINGS FOR FATHERS AND SONS!

FATHER AND SON HAIRCUT DAY PROMOTION

Objective
✄ Reach new male haircut clients.

Description
✄ Offer a free haircut with the purchase of one cut, for dads and sons.

Preparation
✄ **One Month Before**: Make and mail flyers to current client list.

Notify current clients by posting a flyer on your bulletin board for a month previous to the promotion.

Meet with salon staff and explain the promo to everyone. Give all a stack of flyers to distribute.

Make copy of the tracking sheet.

Estimated Cost
✄ $20–30 if only flyers used. Additional cost for postage.

PROMOTION
TRACKING SHEET

(Keep This on a Clipboard at the Reception Desk)

_____
NAME OF PROMOTION

_____   _____
DATE PROMO STARTS   DATE PROMO ENDS

_____
AMOUNT OF NEW CUSTOMERS

	SUN	MON	TUE	WED	THU	FRI	SAT
Week 1							
Week 2							
Week 3							
Week 4							
Monthly Total							

(At the end of every day, take a moment to jot down the number of clients this promotion brought in. At the end of the promotion, total all of the weekly results for a grand total of client responses to this promotion. Be sure to note bad weather, illness, or any mishaps that may have interfered with your promotion's potential success.)

MEMBERS ONLY PROMOTION

Objective
✂ Reach new clients.

Description
✂ Offer a discount to members of any clubs in town.

Preparation
✂ **Two Months Before:** Send letters to tennis clubs, Kiwanis, rotary, junior league, etc.

✂ **One Month Before:** Notify current clients by posting a flyer on your bulletin board.

Meet with salon staff and explain the promo to everyone. Give all a stack of flyers to distribute.

✂ **One Day Before:** Review promo with staff. Make copy of the tracking sheet.

Estimated Cost
✂ $20-30 if only flyers used. Additional cost for postage.

PROMOTION TRACKING SHEET

(Keep This on a Clipboard at the Reception Desk)

_____

NAME OF PROMOTION

_____   _____

DATE PROMO STARTS   DATE PROMO ENDS

_____

AMOUNT OF NEW CUSTOMERS

	SUN	MON	TUE	WED	THU	FRI	SAT
Week 1							
Week 2							
Week 3							
Week 4							
Monthly Total							

(At the end of every day, take a moment to jot down the number of clients this promotion brought in. At the end of the promotion, total all of the weekly results for a grand total of client responses to this promotion. Be sure to note bad weather, illness, or any mishaps that may have interfered with your promotion's potential success.)

Announcing the

"Worst Thing I Ever Did to My Hair Contest"

Salon Name
Address
Phone

Show us the very worst thing
you ever did to your hair…
and we will fix it for you with a
FREE MAKEOVER!

We will do what ever it takes
to repair the winner's hair

Decisions of the judges is final!

THE WORST THING I EVER DID TO MY HAIR PROMOTION

Objective
✂ Reach new clients through a contest.

Description
✂ Offer a contest to save the worst hair in town.

Preparation
✂ **Two Months Before:** Place an ad in newspaper and get copy of the ad slick to use for flyers. (Buy neon paper to run flyers on.)

✂ **One Month Before:** Distribute flyers as bag stuffers (local stores, resorts, hotels, schools). Notify current clients by posting a flyer on your bulletin board for a month previous to the promotion.

Meet with salon staff and explain the promo to everyone. Give all a stack of flyers to distribute.

✂ **One Week Before:** Double check with the newspaper, do a press release.

✂ **One Day Before the Ad Runs:** Review promo with staff. Make copy of the tracking sheet.

Estimated Cost
✂ $20-30 if only flyers used. Additional cost for newspaper ad—depends on ad size and newspaper rates.

PROMOTION TRACKING SHEET

(Keep This on a Clipboard at the Reception Desk)

_____

NAME OF PROMOTION

_____   _____

DATE PROMO STARTS   DATE PROMO ENDS

_____

AMOUNT OF NEW CUSTOMERS

	SUN	MON	TUE	WED	THU	FRI	SAT
Week 1							
Week 2							
Week 3							
Week 4							
Monthly Total							

(At the end of every day, take a moment to jot down the number of clients this promotion brought in. At the end of the promotion, total all of the weekly results for a grand total of client responses to this promotion. Be sure to note bad weather, illness, or any mishaps that may have interfered with your promotion's potential success.)

Jazzy Specials

For when you've got the blues

50% OFF ALL COLOR IN JANUARY

Don't let the dreary winter storms make you blue.

Let us jazz up your winter look with
the color you always wanted.

Salon Name
Address
Phone

Selected Stylists Participating in this Sale

JAZZY SPECIALS FOR WHEN YOU HAVE THE BLUES PROMOTION

Objective
✂ Reach new color clients.

Description
✂ Offer a change from the same old color.

Preparation
✂ **Two Months Before:** Place an ad in newspaper and get copy of the ad slick to use for flyers. (Buy neon paper to run flyers on.)

Check for co-op money with color manufacturers. The company that made the haircolor may offer rebates to help you with the promo cost.

✂ **One Month Before:** Distribute flyers as bag stuffers (local stores, resorts, hotels, schools). Notify current clients by posting a flyer on your bulletin board for a month previous to the promotion.

Meet with salon staff and explain the promo to everyone. Give all a stack of flyers to distribute.

✂ **One Week Before:** Double check with the newspaper, be sure you have enough color.

✂ **One Day Before the Ad Runs:** Review promo with staff. Make copy of the tracking sheet.

Estimated Cost
✂ $20-30 if only flyers used. Additional cost for newspaper ad—depends on ad size and newspaper rates.

PROMOTION TRACKING SHEET

(Keep This on a Clipboard at the Reception Desk)

_____

NAME OF PROMOTION

_____   _____

DATE PROMO STARTS   DATE PROMO ENDS

_____

AMOUNT OF NEW CUSTOMERS

	SUN	MON	TUE	WED	THU	FRI	SAT
Week 1							
Week 2							
Week 3							
Week 4							
Monthly Total							

(At the end of every day, take a moment to jot down the number of clients this promotion brought in. At the end of the promotion, total all of the weekly results for a grand total of client responses to this promotion. Be sure to note bad weather, illness, or any mishaps that may have interfered with your promotion's potential success.)

NEW MOTHERS TREAT

Congratulations!

Salon Name
Address
Phone

Invites all new mothers
to a *FREE* makeover!

We know how busy
new moms can be,
so let us give you a
care-free, no hassle hairstyle

**Your gift from the salon
that wants to baby <u>you</u>!**

NEW MOM MAKEOVERS PROMOTION

Objective
✂ Reach new clients.

Description
✂ Offer a free makeover to new mothers.

Preparation
✂ **One Month Before:** Distribute flyers as letters to hospitals, OB/GYN doctors, etc. Notify current clients by posting a flyer on your bulletin board for a month previous to the promotion.

Meet with salon staff and explain the promo to everyone. Give all a stack of flyers to distribute.

Make copy of the tracking sheet.

Estimated Cost
✂ $20–30 if only flyers used. Additional cost for postage.

PROMOTION TRACKING SHEET

(Keep This on a Clipboard at the Reception Desk)

_____

NAME OF PROMOTION

_____   _____

DATE PROMO STARTS   DATE PROMO ENDS

_____

AMOUNT OF NEW CUSTOMERS

	SUN	MON	TUE	WED	THU	FRI	SAT
Week 1							
Week 2							
Week 3							
Week 4							
Monthly Total							

(At the end of every day, take a moment to jot down the number of clients this promotion brought in. At the end of the promotion, total all of the weekly results for a grand total of client responses to this promotion. Be sure to note bad weather, illness, or any mishaps that may have interfered with your promotion's potential success.)

White Glove Classes For Young Ladies

Salon Name
Address
Phone

Invites young ladies ages 10–15 for FREE "White Glove Classes"

This three-week "finishing school" will give every young lady the poise and grace she will need to succeed in the future.

Classes are free and space is limited.

WHITE GLOVE CLASSES FOR YOUNG LADIES PROMOTION

Objective

✄ Reach new clients. Help young girls gain poise, and confidence in their appearance.

Description

✄ Offer free charm classes on Saturday mornings for 2 or 3 weeks in a row.

Preparation

✄ **Two Months Before:** Place an ad in newspaper and get copy of the ad slick to use for flyers. (Buy neon paper to run flyers on.)

Buy a charm book and brush up on etiquette.

✄ **One Month Before:** Distribute flyers as bag stuffers (local stores, resorts, hotels, schools). Notify current clients by posting a flyer on your bulletin board for a month previous to the promotion.

Meet with salon staff and explain the promo to everyone. Give all a stack of flyers to distribute.

✄ **One Week Before:** Double check with the newspaper. Be sure you have enough mousse, display it in salon.

✄ **One Day Before the Ad Runs:** Review promo with staff. Make copy of the tracking sheet.

Estimated Cost

✄ $20-30 if only flyers used. Additional cost for newspaper ad—depends on ad size and newspaper rates.

PROMOTION TRACKING SHEET

(Keep This on a Clipboard at the Reception Desk)

_____

NAME OF PROMOTION

_____   _____

DATE PROMO STARTS   DATE PROMO ENDS

_____

AMOUNT OF NEW CUSTOMERS

	SUN	MON	TUE	WED	THU	FRI	SAT
Week 1							
Week 2							
Week 3							
Week 4							
Monthly Total							

(At the end of every day, take a moment to jot down the number of clients this promotion brought in. At the end of the promotion, total all of the weekly results for a grand total of client responses to this promotion. Be sure to note bad weather, illness, or any mishaps that may have interfered with your promotion's potential success.)

A Contest for Kids

Win A Prize

Draw a picture of a Thanksgiving Turkey
on this flyer and color the picture.

Salon Name
Phone

We are thankful for **you**!

Contest Ends November 30th

KIDS COLORING CONTEST PROMOTION

Objective

✂ Reach new clients. Reward clients that are kids.

Description

✂ Offer a coloring contest for all kids. Reward all kids who enter. Give out balloons and pencils with salon name on them. Display all artwork in the salon.

Estimated Cost

✂ $20–$30 for flyers used. Additional cost for prizes.

PROMOTION TRACKING SHEET

(Keep This on a Clipboard at the Reception Desk)

_____

NAME OF PROMOTION

_____   _____

DATE PROMO STARTS   DATE PROMO ENDS

_____

AMOUNT OF NEW CUSTOMERS

	SUN	MON	TUE	WED	THU	FRI	SAT
Week 1							
Week 2							
Week 3							
Week 4							
Monthly Total							

(At the end of every day, take a moment to jot down the number of clients this promotion brought in. At the end of the promotion, total all of the weekly results for a grand total of client responses to this promotion. Be sure to note bad weather, illness, or any mishaps that may have interfered with your promotion's potential success.)

Bee Hive Contest!

Show us a photo
of the hairdo you wore
in high school

The best 1950's Beehive
wins a free makeover!

Salon Name
Address
Phone

BEEHIVE CONTEST PROMOTION

Objective
✂ Reach clients and have fun with current ones.

Description
✂ Offer a contest in which clients bring in a photo of themselves in a beehive hairdo.

Preparation
✂ Meet with salon staff and explain the promo to everyone.

Make copies your flyer or make a poster of it to post in the salon. Make copy of the tracking sheet.

Estimated Cost
✂ $20–30 if only flyers used.

PROMOTION
TRACKING SHEET

_____

NAME OF PROMOTION

_____   _____

DATE PROMO STARTS   DATE PROMO ENDS

_____

AMOUNT OF NEW CUSTOMERS

	SUN	MON	TUE	WED	THU	FRI	SAT
Week 1							
Week 2							
Week 3							
Week 4							
Monthly Total							

(At the end of every day, take a moment to jot down the number of clients this promotion brought in. At the end of the promotion, total all of the weekly results for a grand total of client responses to this promotion. Be sure to note bad weather, illness, or any mishaps that may have interfered with your promotion's potential success.)

Career Makeovers For New Grads

**Our Gift to You—
A New Hairstyle
To Suit Your New Career**

Coupon valid June 1- 30, 1997

Salon Name
Phone

Invites New Grads to Enjoy
A *FREE* Makeover!

NEW CAREER MAKEOVERS PROMOTION

Objective
✄ Reach new clients.

Description
✄ Offer a free makeover for all June grads.

Preparation
✄ **One Month Before:** Distribute flyers as handouts at rehearsals for local graduation ceremonies (call schools and get permission). Notify current clients by posting a flyer on your bulletin board for a month previous to the promotion.

Meet with salon staff and explain the promo to everyone. Give all a stack of flyers to distribute. Make copy of the tracking sheet.

Estimated Cost
✄ $20-30 if only flyers used.

PROMOTION TRACKING SHEET

(Keep This on a Clipboard at the Reception Desk)

_____

NAME OF PROMOTION

_____   _____

DATE PROMO STARTS   DATE PROMO ENDS

_____

AMOUNT OF NEW CUSTOMERS

	SUN	MON	TUE	WED	THU	FRI	SAT
Week 1							
Week 2							
Week 3							
Week 4							
Monthly Total							

(At the end of every day, take a moment to jot down the number of clients this promotion brought in. At the end of the promotion, total all of the weekly results for a grand total of client responses to this promotion. Be sure to note bad weather, illness, or any mishaps that may have interfered with your promotion's potential success.)

May We Suggest A Day of Beauty?

A DAY OF BEAUTY GIFT CERTIFICATE

We are your pot of gold at the end of the rainbow.

Someone loves you so very much, that they have purchased a day of beauty especially for you.

You may use this certificate for all services you would like to try!

THIS GIFT IS FROM:

_____

_____

Start With a Manicure and Pedicure,
Add a Facial and Perm!

You Could Even Try a New Color!

Salon Name
Phone

A DAY OF BEAUTY GIFT CERTIFICATE PROMOTION

Objective
✁ Reach new clients.

Description
✁ Sell gift certificates for holiday gift giving.

Preparation
✁ Create gift certificates like the one attached. Post them in the salon and sell them at half-price.

Meet with salon staff and explain the promo to everyone. Tell them to suggest them as birthday gifts, mother's day treats, and secretary's day awards.

Estimated cost
✁ $20–30 if only flyers used.

PROMOTION
TRACKING SHEET

(Keep This on a Clipboard at the Reception Desk)

_____

NAME OF PROMOTION

_____   _____

DATE PROMO STARTS   DATE PROMO ENDS

_____

AMOUNT OF NEW CUSTOMERS

	SUN	MON	TUE	WED	THU	FRI	SAT
Week 1							
Week 2							
Week 3							
Week 4							
Monthly Total							

(At the end of every day, take a moment to jot down the number of clients this promotion brought in. At the end of the promotion, total all of the weekly results for a grand total of client responses to this promotion. Be sure to note bad weather, illness, or any mishaps that may have interfered with your promotion's potential success.)

Salon Name
Phone

Any service that contains a red, white or blue color is *half-price*!

Including:
Red Hair Color
Red or Blue Nail Polish
Blue Rinses
French Manicures

All haircuts are half-price too!

This Sale is an All-American Blast!

July 1–5 only

RED, WHITE AND BLUE SALE PROMOTION

Objective
ै<Reach new clients.

Description
ै<Offer a sale on all services that are red, white, or blue, and on haircuts.

Preparation
ै< **Two Months Before:** Place an ad in newspaper and get copy of the ad slick to use for flyers. (Buy neon paper to run flyers on.)

ै< **One Month Before:** Distribute flyers as bag stuffers (stores, resorts, hotels, schools). Notify current clients by posting a flyer on your bulletin board for a month previous to the promotion.

Meet with salon staff and explain the promo to everyone. Give all a stack of flyers to distribute.

ै< **One Week Before:** Double check with the newspaper.

ै< **One Day Before the Ad Runs:** Review promo with staff. Make copy of the tracking sheet.

Estimated Cost
ै< $20-30 if only flyers used. Additional cost for newspaper ad—depends on ad size and newspaper rates.

PROMOTION TRACKING SHEET

(Keep This on a Clipboard at the Reception Desk)

_____

NAME OF PROMOTION

_____   _____

DATE PROMO STARTS   DATE PROMO ENDS

_____

AMOUNT OF NEW CUSTOMERS

	SUN	MON	TUE	WED	THU	FRI	SAT
Week 1							
Week 2							
Week 3							
Week 4							
Monthly Total							

(At the end of every day, take a moment to jot down the number of clients this promotion brought in. At the end of the promotion, total all of the weekly results for a grand total of client responses to this promotion. Be sure to note bad weather, illness, or any mishaps that may have interfered with your promotion's potential success.)

Cowgirls Two Step Sale

Step Into Our Salon,
Two Cowgirls at a Time and
We Will Give You
Two Haircuts
FOR THE PRICE OF ONE!

Salon Name
Address
Phone

Y'all come in for this special in May 1998!

COWGIRLS TWO STEP PROMOTION

Objective:

✂ Reach new clients.

Description

✂ Offer a free haircut with the purchase of one cut.

Preparation

✂ **Two Months Before:** Place an ad in newspaper and get copy of the ad slick to use for flyers. (Buy neon paper to run flyers on.)

✂ **One Month Before:** Distribute flyers as bag stuffers (western stores, night clubs, dance schools). Notify current clients by posting a flyer on your bulletin board for a month previous to the promotion.

Meet with salon staff and explain the promo to everyone. Give all a stack of flyers to distribute.

✂ **One Week Before:** Double check with the newspaper.

✂ **One Day Before the Ad Runs:** Review promo with staff. Make copy of the tracking sheet.

Estimated Cost

✂ $20~30 if only flyers used. Additional cost for newspaper ad—depends on ad size and newspaper rates.

PROMOTION
TRACKING SHEET

(Keep This on a Clipboard at the Reception Desk)

_____

NAME OF PROMOTION

_____   _____

DATE PROMO STARTS   DATE PROMO ENDS

_____

AMOUNT OF NEW CUSTOMERS

	SUN	MON	TUE	WED	THU	FRI	SAT
Week 1							
Week 2							
Week 3							
Week 4							
Monthly Total							

(At the end of every day, take a moment to jot down the number of clients this promotion brought in. At the end of the promotion, total all of the weekly results for a grand total of client responses to this promotion. Be sure to note bad weather, illness, or any mishaps that may have interfered with your promotion's potential success.)

May Day Makeovers

Visit Our Salon on May Day
and
Let Us Make You Over
For Spring

Salon Name
Address
Phone

Let us get you ready for
all the new Spring fashions!

We will even give you

$5 off any service

on May Day

Call for your appointment today!

MAY DAY MAKEOVERS PROMOTION

Objective
✄ Reach new clients.

Description
✄ Offer a $5 savings on a makeover on May Day.

Preparation
✄ Create your own flyer and mail it to client list.

✄ **One Month Before:** Distribute flyers as bag stuffers to stores, clubs, offices and schools. Notify current clients by posting a flyer on your bulletin board for a month previous to the promotion.

Meet with salon staff and explain the promo to everyone. Give all a stack of flyers to distribute.

Make copy of the tracking sheet.

Estimated Cost
✄ $20-30 if only flyers used. Additional cost for postage.

PROMOTION TRACKING SHEET

(Keep This on a Clipboard at the Reception Desk)

NAME OF PROMOTION

DATE PROMO STARTS

DATE PROMO ENDS

AMOUNT OF NEW CUSTOMERS

	SUN	MON	TUE	WED	THU	FRI	SAT
Week 1							
Week 2							
Week 3							
Week 4							
Monthly Total							

(At the end of every day, take a moment to jot down the number of clients this promotion brought in. At the end of the promotion, total all of the weekly results for a grand total of client responses to this promotion. Be sure to note bad weather, illness, or any mishaps that may have interfered with your promotion's potential success.)

Architects Know It...

_____

Scientists Know It...

_____

Hairstylists Know It...

_____

Form is Determined by Function

The form of your haircut, should be determined by the
function you would like it to perform...
A quick and easy "sporty" look or a tailored, sophisticated
style: Let us give you a haircut that fits the function!

Salon Name
Address
Phone

FORM DETERMINES FUNCTION PROMOTION

Objective

✄ Reach haircut clients.

Description

✄ Send this flyer to scientists, engineers, and doctors. One of the basic rules of physics is: form is determined by function. Engineers build a building to suit your needs and as a hairstylist you will create a cut that is determined by their needs!

Preparation

✄ Notify current clients by posting a flyer on your bulletin board for a month previous to the promotion.

Meet with salon staff and explain the promo to everyone. Give all a stack of flyers to distribute.

Make copy of the tracking sheet.

Estimated Cost

✄ $20–30 if only flyers used. Additional cost for postage.

PROMOTION
TRACKING SHEET

(Keep This on a Clipboard at the Reception Desk)

_____

NAME OF PROMOTION

_____   _____

DATE PROMO STARTS   DATE PROMO ENDS

_____

AMOUNT OF NEW CUSTOMERS

	SUN	MON	TUE	WED	THU	FRI	SAT
Week 1							
Week 2							
Week 3							
Week 4							
Monthly Total							

(At the end of every day, take a moment to jot down the number of clients this promotion brought in. At the end of the promotion, total all of the weekly results for a grand total of client responses to this promotion. Be sure to note bad weather, illness, or any mishaps that may have interfered with your promotion's potential success.)

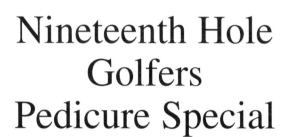

Nineteenth Hole Golfers Pedicure Special

$5 Off *Any Pedicure*

Salon Name
Phone

NINETEENTH HOLE PEDICURE PROMOTION

Objective
✄ Reach new pedicure clients from local golf clubs and sporting good stores.

Description
✄ Offer $5 off a pedicure to all golfers.

Preparation
✄ **Two Months Before:** Place an ad in newspaper and get copy of the ad slick to use for flyers. (Buy neon paper to run flyers on.)

✄ **One Month Before:** Distribute flyers at golf clubs and sporting good stores, resorts, hotels, schools. Notify current clients by posting a flyer on your bulletin board for a month previous to the promotion.

Meet with salon staff and explain the promo to everyone. Give all a stack of flyers to distribute.

✄ **One Week Before:** Double check with the newspaper.

✄ **One Day Before the Ad Runs:** Review promo with staff. Make copy of the tracking sheet.

Estimated Cost
✄ $20-30 if only flyers used. Additional cost for newspaper ad—depends on ad size and newspaper rates.

PROMOTION TRACKING SHEET

(Keep This on a Clipboard at the Reception Desk)

_____

NAME OF PROMOTION

_____   _____

DATE PROMO STARTS   DATE PROMO ENDS

_____

AMOUNT OF NEW CUSTOMERS

	SUN	MON	TUE	WED	THU	FRI	SAT
Week 1							
Week 2							
Week 3							
Week 4							
Monthly Total							

(At the end of every day, take a moment to jot down the number of clients this promotion brought in. At the end of the promotion, total all of the weekly results for a grand total of client responses to this promotion. Be sure to note bad weather, illness, or any mishaps that may have interfered with your promotion's potential success.)

Free Nail Art Today!

Salon Name
Address • Phone

Try One FREE Nail Of Nail Art

Gems and Stripes or Airbrush

Meet Our Newest
Nail Technician
(place technician's name here)

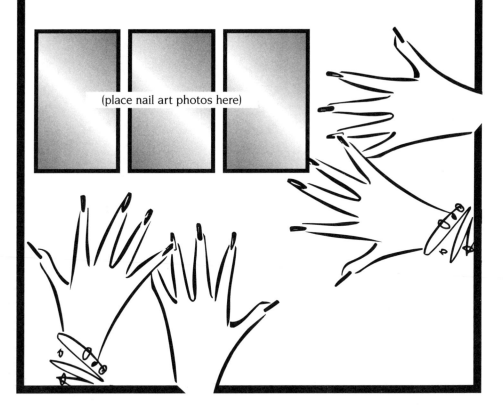

(place nail art photos here)

NAIL ART PROMOTION

Objective
✄ Reach new nail clients.

Description
✄ Offer one free nail of nail art.

Preparation
✄ Make a poster of nail art and a photo of your newest nail tech. Post it in the salon every Saturday for a month. Be sure to have a variety of gems and stripes on hand, as well as paint for the airbrush.

Estimated Cost
✄ Get quotes for the poster and take the photos yourself (consider film).

PROMOTION TRACKING SHEET

(Keep This on a Clipboard at the Reception Desk)

_____

NAME OF PROMOTION

_____   _____

DATE PROMO STARTS   DATE PROMO ENDS

_____

AMOUNT OF NEW CUSTOMERS

	SUN	MON	TUE	WED	THU	FRI	SAT
Week 1							
Week 2							
Week 3							
Week 4							
Monthly Total							

(At the end of every day, take a moment to jot down the number of clients this promotion brought in. At the end of the promotion, total all of the weekly results for a grand total of client responses to this promotion. Be sure to note bad weather, illness, or any mishaps that may have interfered with your promotion's potential success.)

FREE
Nail Wrap Today

Salon Name

Try one **FREE** nail of nail wrapping!

Strengthen your natural nails!

This is the perfect service after you remove the tips!

Place nail wrap photo here

Meet our newest nail technician
(Place technician's name here)

WRAP IT UP PROMOTION

Objective
✄ Reach new nail clients.

Description
✄ Offer one free nail wrap.

Preparation
✄ Make a poster of nail wrappings photos and a photo of your newest nail tech. Post it in the salon every Saturday for a month. Be sure to have a variety of wrap product on hand.

Estimated Cost
✄ Get estimates on poster prices.

PROMOTION TRACKING SHEET

(Keep This on a Clipboard at the Reception Desk)

_____

NAME OF PROMOTION

_____   _____

DATE PROMO STARTS   DATE PROMO ENDS

_____

AMOUNT OF NEW CUSTOMERS

	SUN	MON	TUE	WED	THU	FRI	SAT
Week 1							
Week 2							
Week 3							
Week 4							
Monthly Total							

(At the end of every day, take a moment to jot down the number of clients this promotion brought in. At the end of the promotion, total all of the weekly results for a grand total of client responses to this promotion. Be sure to note bad weather, illness, or any mishaps that may have interfered with your promotion's potential success.)

We Are
The Teacher's Pet
Salon Name
Address • Phone

We love teachers and we want to give them a

HALF-PRICE HAIRCUT

For a back to school gift!

Stop in any Monday in September

for your *half-price* haircut!

Walk Ins Only

Selected Stylists

TEACHER'S PET PROMOTION

Objective
✂ Reach new haircut clients.

Description
✂ Offer a sale for teachers, in September.

Preparation
✂ Make a copy of your flyer and mail it to every school in your town.

Meet with staff and explain the promotion.

Estimated Cost
✂ $20–30 for flyers, plus postage

PROMOTION TRACKING SHEET

(Keep This on a Clipboard at the Reception Desk)

_____

NAME OF PROMOTION

_____   _____

DATE PROMO STARTS   DATE PROMO ENDS

_____

AMOUNT OF NEW CUSTOMERS

	SUN	MON	TUE	WED	THU	FRI	SAT
Week 1							
Week 2							
Week 3							
Week 4							
Monthly Total							

(At the end of every day, take a moment to jot down the number of clients this promotion brought in. At the end of the promotion, total all of the weekly results for a grand total of client responses to this promotion. Be sure to note bad weather, illness, or any mishaps that may have interfered with your promotion's potential success.)

Special Haircare For Swimmers

It's okay to swim in pools, but you must take special care of your hair!

We offer special haircare for swimmers!

Chlorine can damage your hair, but we are specialists in repairing your hair.

Special treatments, conditioners, shampoos, and haircuts can take the hassle out of swimming in pools.

Try a "Wash & Wear Haircut"

Call Us Today!

Salon Name
Phone

SWIMMERS SPECIALS PROMOTION

Objective
✂ Reach new haircut, conditioner and retail clients. Help clients save hair from chlorine abuse.

Description
✂ Offer special attention to swimmers' hair needs.

Preparation
✂ **Two Months Before:** Place an ad in newspaper and get copy of the ad slick to use for flyers. (Buy neon paper to run flyers on.)

Stock several cases of retail for swimmers.

✂ **One Month Before:** Distribute flyers as bag stuffers (swimsuit stores, resorts, beach hotels, pools). Notify current clients by posting a flyer on your bulletin board for a month previous to the promotion.

Meet with salon staff and explain the promo to everyone. Give all a stack of flyers to distribute.

✂ **One Week Before:** Double check with the newspaper.

✂ **One Day Before the Ad Runs:** Review promo with staff. Make copy of the tracking sheet.

Estimated Cost
✂ $20–30 if only flyers used. Additional cost for newspaper ad—depends on ad size and newspaper rates. Also, remember to allocate additional retail money to stock up on shampoo and conditioners.

PROMOTION TRACKING SHEET

(Keep This on a Clipboard at the Reception Desk)

_____

NAME OF PROMOTION

_____   _____

DATE PROMO STARTS   DATE PROMO ENDS

_____

AMOUNT OF NEW CUSTOMERS

	SUN	MON	TUE	WED	THU	FRI	SAT
Week 1							
Week 2							
Week 3							
Week 4							
Monthly Total							

(At the end of every day, take a moment to jot down the number of clients this promotion brought in. At the end of the promotion, total all of the weekly results for a grand total of client responses to this promotion. Be sure to note bad weather, illness, or any mishaps that may have interfered with your promotion's potential success.)

SKI CLUB PROMOTION

Objective
✄ Reach new clients.

Description
✄ Offer a treatment to ski-damaged hair clients.

Preparation
✄ Create your promo, make copies, and mail it to all ski clubs and stores in the area.

Notify current clients by posting a flyer on your bulletin board for a month previous to the promotion.

Meet with salon staff and explain the promo to everyone. Give all a stack of flyers to distribute.

Make copy of the tracking sheet.

Estimated Cost
✄ $20–30 if only flyers used. Additional cost for postage.

PROMOTION TRACKING SHEET

(Keep This on a Clipboard at the Reception Desk)

_____

NAME OF PROMOTION

_____   _____

DATE PROMO STARTS   DATE PROMO ENDS

_____

AMOUNT OF NEW CUSTOMERS

	SUN	MON	TUE	WED	THU	FRI	SAT
Week 1							
Week 2							
Week 3							
Week 4							
Monthly Total							

(At the end of every day, take a moment to jot down the number of clients this promotion brought in. At the end of the promotion, total all of the weekly results for a grand total of client responses to this promotion. Be sure to note bad weather, illness, or any mishaps that may have interfered with your promotion's potential success.)

Salesclerks Are Special

At:
Salon Name
Phone

We Offer Salesclerks a
FREE Haircut!

We will cut and style your hair
FREE this week.

In exchange, we will ask you
to wear a small tag that says:
"ASK ME ABOUT MY HAIR"

(Every time someone asks you about your hair, give her one of our cards
with your name on it. Every time two cards come back
with your name on them, you win a free haircut!)

You Could Win **FREE** Cuts All Year

SALESCLERK PROMOTION

Objective
✂ Reach new clients.

Description
✂ Offer a free cut in exchange for wearing a name tag that says that you cut their hair. Also, they can hand out your business card, with their name on the back of it, when two cards are turned in, they win a free haircut.

Preparation
✂ Make copies of your flyer and distribute it to store managers in your area. Meet with salon staff and explain the promo to everyone. Make copy of the tracking sheet.

Estimated Cost
✂ $20-30 if only flyers used. Additional cost for postage.

PROMOTION TRACKING SHEET

(Keep This on a Clipboard at the Reception Desk)

_____

NAME OF PROMOTION

_____   _____

DATE PROMO STARTS   DATE PROMO ENDS

_____

AMOUNT OF NEW CUSTOMERS

	SUN	MON	TUE	WED	THU	FRI	SAT
Week 1							
Week 2							
Week 3							
Week 4							
Monthly Total							

(At the end of every day, take a moment to jot down the number of clients this promotion brought in. At the end of the promotion, total all of the weekly results for a grand total of client responses to this promotion. Be sure to note bad weather, illness, or any mishaps that may have interfered with your promotion's potential success.)

Wedding Party—Makeover Party

SALON NAME
ADDRESS
PHONE

WILL HOLD A MAKEOVER PARTY FOR YOUR WEDDING PARTY!

WHY STOP AT JUST DRESSING WELL FOR THE WEDDING?

LET US HELP ALL MEMBERS OF THE WEDDING PARTY LOOK THEIR BEST!

LET'S TRY NEW HAIRSTYLES AND MAKEUP FOR THE SPECIAL DAY.

NAIL SERVICES AVAILABLE, TOO!

GET A NEW LOOK FOR ALL THE MEMBERS OF YOUR WEDDING PARTY!

MAKEOVER PARTY FOR THE WEDDING PARTY PROMOTION

Objective

✂ Reach new clients.

Description

✂ Offer a makeover party for wedding parties. Watch for engagement notices in the newspaper and send the couples a congratulatory card and a copy of your flyer.

Preparation

✂ Make copies of your flyer and buy congratulation cards.

Meet with salon staff and explain the promo to everyone. Make copy of the tracking sheet.

Estimated Cost

✂ $20–30 if only flyers used. Additional cost for cards and postage.

PROMOTION TRACKING SHEET

(Keep This on a Clipboard at the Reception Desk)

_____

NAME OF PROMOTION

_____   _____

DATE PROMO STARTS   DATE PROMO ENDS

_____

AMOUNT OF NEW CUSTOMERS

	SUN	MON	TUE	WED	THU	FRI	SAT
Week 1							
Week 2							
Week 3							
Week 4							
Monthly Total							

(At the end of every day, take a moment to jot down the number of clients this promotion brought in. At the end of the promotion, total all of the weekly results for a grand total of client responses to this promotion. Be sure to note bad weather, illness, or any mishaps that may have interfered with your promotion's potential success.)

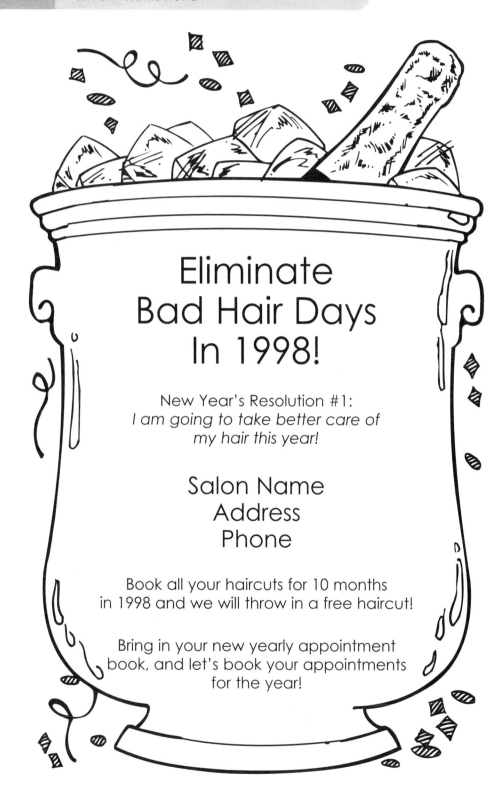

Eliminate Bad Hair Days In 1998!

New Year's Resolution #1:
I am going to take better care of my hair this year!

Salon Name
Address
Phone

Book all your haircuts for 10 months
in 1998 and we will throw in a free haircut!

Bring in your new yearly appointment
book, and let's book your appointments
for the year!

BOOK A YEAR'S CUTS AND SAVE PROMOTION

Objective

✀ Book current clients for the entire year.

Description

✀ Offer a free haircut after they book and have 10 cuts for next year.

Preparation

✀ Make a poster and post in the salon. Meet with salon staff and explain the promo to everyone.

Estimated Cost

✀ $3 for poster

PROMOTION TRACKING SHEET

(Keep This on a Clipboard at the Reception Desk)

_____

NAME OF PROMOTION

_____   _____

DATE PROMO STARTS   DATE PROMO ENDS

_____

AMOUNT OF NEW CUSTOMERS

	SUN	MON	TUE	WED	THU	FRI	SAT
Week 1							
Week 2							
Week 3							
Week 4							
Monthly Total							

(At the end of every day, take a moment to jot down the number of clients this promotion brought in. At the end of the promotion, total all of the weekly results for a grand total of client responses to this promotion. Be sure to note bad weather, illness, or any mishaps that may have interfered with your promotion's potential success.)

IT IS IN THE BAG!

PROTECT YOUR INVESTMENT AND HELP YOUR PERMS LAST LONGER

DON'T HAVE A PERM TODAY AND FORGET TO PURCHASE YOUR HOME HAIRCARE PRODUCTS!

THE MAJOR CAUSE OF PERMS NOT LASTING LONG ENOUGH, IS THE USE OF THE WRONG PRODUCTS TO MAINTAIN THE PERM!

WE HAVE A FULL LINE OF SHAMPOOS, CONDITIONERS, TREATMENTS AND SUNSCREENS SPECIFICALLY FORMULATED TO HELP YOUR PERM LAST LONGER.

SALON NAME

ADDRESS

PHONE

Here Is $3 To Use Toward Any Retail Purchase Made Today!

$3 OFF $3 OFF

IT IS IN THE BAG PROMOTION

Objective
✂ Reach new retail clients and help perms last longer! Reduce perm re-dos from abuse.

Description
✂ Offer a $3 discount on all perm retail products to all clients who purchase a perm. Copy your flyer and give it to every perm client.

Preparation
✂ This should be an on-going promotion. Meet with salon staff and explain the promo to everyone.

Estimated Cost
✂ $20–30 if only flyers used.

PROMOTION TRACKING SHEET

(Keep This on a Clipboard at the Reception Desk)

_____

NAME OF PROMOTION

_____   _____

DATE PROMO STARTS   DATE PROMO ENDS

_____

AMOUNT OF NEW CUSTOMERS

	SUN	MON	TUE	WED	THU	FRI	SAT
Week 1							
Week 2							
Week 3							
Week 4							
Monthly Total							

(At the end of every day, take a moment to jot down the number of clients this promotion brought in. At the end of the promotion, total all of the weekly results for a grand total of client responses to this promotion. Be sure to note bad weather, illness, or any mishaps that may have interfered with your promotion's potential success.)

How to Manage That Mane

Ever feel like your hair is looking
a lot like a lion's mane?

Help Is Here!

Let us tame your mane!

We have a new collection of haircuts especially
designed to help unruly hair be tamed!

We have the latest shampoos and conditioners
to calm the savage beast in anyone's tresses!

Salon Name
Address
Phone

Call Us Today!

A $5 Coupon
to Help You Get
a Handle on
Your Hair!

MANAGE THAT MANE PROMOTION

Objective
✂ Reach new cut and retail clients.

Description
✂ Offer a discount coupon to try your salon.

Preparation
✂ **Two Months Before:** Place an ad in newspaper and get copy of the ad slick to use for flyers. (Buy neon paper to run flyers on.)

✂ **One Month Before:** Distribute flyers as bag stuffers (stores, resorts, hotels, schools). Notify current clients by posting a flyer on your bulletin board for a month previous to the promotion.

Meet with salon staff and explain the promo to everyone. Give all a stack of flyers to distribute.

✂ **One Week Before:** Double check with the newspaper.

✂ **One Day Before the Ad Runs:** Review promo with staff. Make copy of the tracking sheet.

Estimated Cost
✂ $20-30 if only flyers used. Additional cost for newspaper ad—depends on ad size and newspaper rates.

PROMOTION TRACKING SHEET

(Keep This on a Clipboard at the Reception Desk)

_____

NAME OF PROMOTION

_____   _____

DATE PROMO STARTS   DATE PROMO ENDS

_____

AMOUNT OF NEW CUSTOMERS

	SUN	MON	TUE	WED	THU	FRI	SAT
Week 1							
Week 2							
Week 3							
Week 4							
Monthly Total							

(At the end of every day, take a moment to jot down the number of clients this promotion brought in. At the end of the promotion, total all of the weekly results for a grand total of client responses to this promotion. Be sure to note bad weather, illness, or any mishaps that may have interfered with your promotion's potential success.)

FIRST DAY OF SCHOOL, CUTS ON THE HOUSE PROMOTION

Objective

✁Reach new families as clients.

Description

✁Offer a free haircut to the first 25 kids who make appointments for cuts before their first day of school.

Preparation

✁**Two Months Before**: Place an ad in newspaper and get copy of the ad slick to use for flyers. (Buy neon paper to run flyers on.)

✁**One Month Before**: Distribute flyers as bag stuffers (children's stores, toy stores, and schools). Notify current clients by posting a flyer on your bulletin board for a month previous to the promotion.

Meet with salon staff and explain the promo to everyone. Give all a stack of flyers to distribute.

✁**One Week Before**: Double check with the newspaper.

✁**One Day Before the Ad Runs**: Review promo with staff. Make copy of the tracking sheet.

Estimated Cost

✁$20–30 if only flyers used. Additional cost for newspaper ad—depends on ad size and newspaper rates.

PROMOTION
TRACKING SHEET

(Keep This on a Clipboard at the Reception Desk)

_____
NAME OF PROMOTION

_____   _____
DATE PROMO STARTS   DATE PROMO ENDS

_____
AMOUNT OF NEW CUSTOMERS

	SUN	MON	TUE	WED	THU	FRI	SAT
Week 1							
Week 2							
Week 3							
Week 4							
Monthly Total							

(At the end of every day, take a moment to jot down the number of clients this promotion brought in. At the end of the promotion, total all of the weekly results for a grand total of client responses to this promotion. Be sure to note bad weather, illness, or any mishaps that may have interfered with your promotion's potential success.)

Frequent Haircut Card

Get This Card Punched Every Time We Cut Your Hair

FREQUENT HAIRCUT CARD

① ⑥
② ⑦
③ ⑧
④ ⑨
⑤ ⑩

When You Have **10 PUNCHES** Your Next Haircut is **FREE**

Salon Name
Phone

FREQUENT HAIRCUT CARD PROMOTION

Objective
✂ Inspire haircut clients to return to you.

Description
✂ Offer a free cut when the card is punched 10 times.

Preparation
✂ Make copies of your promo and give to haircut clients.

Meet with salon staff and explain the promo to everyone. Give all a stack of flyers to distribute.

Make copy of the tracking sheet.

Estimated Cost
✂ $20-30 if only flyers used.

PROMOTION TRACKING SHEET

(Keep This on a Clipboard at the Reception Desk)

_____

NAME OF PROMOTION

_____   _____

DATE PROMO STARTS   DATE PROMO ENDS

_____

AMOUNT OF NEW CUSTOMERS

	SUN	MON	TUE	WED	THU	FRI	SAT
Week 1							
Week 2							
Week 3							
Week 4							
Monthly Total							

(At the end of every day, take a moment to jot down the number of clients this promotion brought in. At the end of the promotion, total all of the weekly results for a grand total of client responses to this promotion. Be sure to note bad weather, illness, or any mishaps that may have interfered with your promotion's potential success.)

FIX IT DAY!

This Monday is Fix It Day for Your Hair

New Styles, Colors, and Perms Come and Go,
If:
You Tried It and You Hate It!
Let's Get Rid of It!

Free Workshop and Consultation Day!

Space is Limited
Call Now!

Don't be frustrated with hair that you hate...
Let us fix it for you!

Salon Name
Address
Phone

FIX IT DAY PROMOTION

Objective
✂ Reach new hair and retail clients.

Description
✂ Offer a free consultation and workshop day to repair hair that clients hate!

Preparation
✂ **Two Months Before:** Place an ad in newspaper and get copy of the ad slick to use for flyers. (Buy neon paper to run flyers on.)

✂ **One Month Before:** Distribute flyers as bag stuffers (stores, resorts, hotels, schools, and offices). Notify current clients by posting a flyer on your bulletin board for a month previous to the promotion.

Meet with salon staff and explain the promo to everyone. Give all a stack of flyers to distribute.

✂ **One Week Before:** Double check with the newspaper.

✂ **One Day Before the Ad Runs:** Review promo with staff. Make copy of the tracking sheet.

Estimated Cost
✂ $20-30 if only flyers used. Additional cost for newspaper ad—depends on ad size and newspaper rates.

PROMOTION TRACKING SHEET

(Keep This on a Clipboard at the Reception Desk)

_____

NAME OF PROMOTION

_____   _____

DATE PROMO STARTS   DATE PROMO ENDS

_____

AMOUNT OF NEW CUSTOMERS

	SUN	MON	TUE	WED	THU	FRI	SAT
Week 1							
Week 2							
Week 3							
Week 4							
Monthly Total							

(At the end of every day, take a moment to jot down the number of clients this promotion brought in. At the end of the promotion, total all of the weekly results for a grand total of client responses to this promotion. Be sure to note bad weather, illness, or any mishaps that may have interfered with your promotion's potential success.)

WIG CARE WEEK

This Is Wig Care Week At: (Salon Name)

Bring in your wigs and we will restyle them at *half-price*

(Let us update your investment)

(Photo here of you, styling a wig on a block)

Salon Name

Address

Phone

WIG CARE WEEK PROMOTION

Objective
✄ Reach new hairpiece clients.

Description
✄ Offer a discount to bring in wigs this week.

Preparation
✄ Distribute flyers as bag stuffers to stores, resorts, retirement communities. Notify current clients by posting a flyer on your bulletin board for a month previous to the promotion.

Meet with salon staff and explain the promo to everyone. Give all a stack of flyers to distribute.

Make copy of the tracking sheet.

Estimated Cost
✄ $20-30 if only flyers used. Additional cost for postage if mailed out.

PROMOTION TRACKING SHEET

(Keep This on a Clipboard at the Reception Desk)

_____
NAME OF PROMOTION

_____   _____
DATE PROMO STARTS   DATE PROMO ENDS

_____
AMOUNT OF NEW CUSTOMERS

	SUN	MON	TUE	WED	THU	FRI	SAT
Week 1							
Week 2							
Week 3							
Week 4							
Monthly Total							

(At the end of every day, take a moment to jot down the number of clients this promotion brought in. At the end of the promotion, total all of the weekly results for a grand total of client responses to this promotion. Be sure to note bad weather, illness, or any mishaps that may have interfered with your promotion's potential success.)

Prom Day Promotions

School Name
Is Invited To
A Prom Day Fashion Show!

Salon Name
Address
Phone
Date: Time:

Prom Fashions by: (*store name here*)

Let Us show You the Hottest Looks in Hair, Nails, and Makeup for This Prom Season!

SALON NAME

PROM DAY PROMOTION

Objective
✂ Reach new service and retail clients.

Description
✂ Offer a free fashion show for every school in your during a two week span, before the prom. Team up with a local retailer to provide the dresses.

Preparation
✂ **Two Months Before:** Call local schools and offer the free promotion. Make copies of your promo to hand out at the schools. Meet with salon staff and explain the promo to everyone.

Estimated Cost
✂ $20–30 if only flyers used.

PROMOTION TRACKING SHEET

(Keep This on a Clipboard at the Reception Desk)

_____

NAME OF PROMOTION

_____   _____

DATE PROMO STARTS   DATE PROMO ENDS

_____

AMOUNT OF NEW CUSTOMERS

	SUN	MON	TUE	WED	THU	FRI	SAT
Week 1							
Week 2							
Week 3							
Week 4							
Monthly Total							

(At the end of every day, take a moment to jot down the number of clients this promotion brought in. At the end of the promotion, total all of the weekly results for a grand total of client responses to this promotion. Be sure to note bad weather, illness, or any mishaps that may have interfered with your promotion's potential success.)

A Glamour Makeover Day!

(Date)

Salon Name
and
Photographer's Name

Will offer glamour makeovers
and photos

FOR ONLY $25!

Call For an Appointment Today!

Salon Name
Phone

We Create Works of Art!

PHOTO FINISH—GLAMOUR MAKEOVER PROMOTION

Objective
✂ Reach clients.

Description
✂ Offer a $25 glamour shot. Team up with a photographer in the area.

Preparation
✂ **Two Months Before:** Place an ad in newspaper and get copy of the ad slick to use for flyers. (Buy neon paper to run flyers on.)

✂ **One Month Before:** Distribute flyers as bag stuffers (stores, resorts, hotels, schools). Notify current clients by posting a flyer on your bulletin board for a month previous to the promotion.

Meet with salon staff and explain the promo to everyone. Give all a stack of flyers to distribute.

✂ **One Week Before:** Double check with the newspaper.

✂ **One Day Before the Ad Runs:** Review promo with staff. Make copy of the tracking sheet.

Estimated Cost
✂ $20-30 if only flyers used. Additional cost for newspaper ad—depends on ad size and newspaper rates.

PROMOTION TRACKING SHEET

(Keep This on a Clipboard at the Reception Desk)

_____

NAME OF PROMOTION

_____   _____

DATE PROMO STARTS   DATE PROMO ENDS

_____

AMOUNT OF NEW CUSTOMERS

	SUN	MON	TUE	WED	THU	FRI	SAT
Week 1							
Week 2							
Week 3							
Week 4							
Monthly Total							

(At the end of every day, take a moment to jot down the number of clients this promotion brought in. At the end of the promotion, total all of the weekly results for a grand total of client responses to this promotion. Be sure to note bad weather, illness, or any mishaps that may have interfered with your promotion's potential success.)

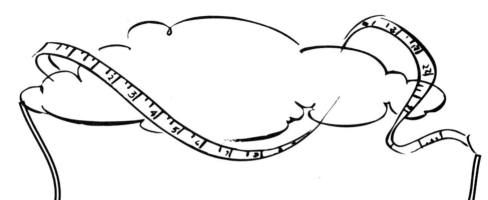

Dieter's Reward

Reach Your Goal At:
(Diet Center's Name Here)

and
Salon Name
Address
Phone

Will Reward You With
A FREE Makeover

Congratulations!
You Are A Winner!

DIETER'S REWARD—REACH YOUR GOAL PROMOTION

Objective

✂ Reach new clients.

Description

✂ Offer a free makeover to dieters who reach goal!

Preparation

✂ Meet with local diet centers and offer the promo to them. Ask them to help with the flyer distribution.

Meet with salon staff and explain the promo to everyone. Give all a stack of flyers to distribute.

Make copy of the tracking sheet.

Estimated Cost

✂ $20–30 if only flyers used.

PROMOTION TRACKING SHEET

(Keep This on a Clipboard at the Reception Desk)

_____

NAME OF PROMOTION

_____   _____

DATE PROMO STARTS   DATE PROMO ENDS

_____

AMOUNT OF NEW CUSTOMERS

	SUN	MON	TUE	WED	THU	FRI	SAT
Week 1							
Week 2							
Week 3							
Week 4							
Monthly Total							

(At the end of every day, take a moment to jot down the number of clients this promotion brought in. At the end of the promotion, total all of the weekly results for a grand total of client responses to this promotion. Be sure to note bad weather, illness, or any mishaps that may have interfered with your promotion's potential success.)

ENGAGEMENT RING GIFT

PRESENT THIS CARD FOR A FREE MANICURE

SALON NAME
Address
Phone

ENGAGEMENT RING PROMOTION

Objective

✂ Reach new clients.

Description

✂ Offer a free manicure to everyone who buys an engagement ring from a jeweler who has agreed to help you with the promotion.

Preparation

✂ Print up little cards that the jeweler can give each client that buys a ring. Meet with salon staff and explain the promo to everyone. Make copy of the tracking sheet.

Estimated Cost

✂ $20–30 if only cards used.

PROMOTION TRACKING SHEET

(Keep This on a Clipboard at the Reception Desk)

_____
NAME OF PROMOTION

_____   _____
DATE PROMO STARTS   DATE PROMO ENDS

_____
AMOUNT OF NEW CUSTOMERS

	SUN	MON	TUE	WED	THU	FRI	SAT
Week 1							
Week 2							
Week 3							
Week 4							
Monthly Total							

(At the end of every day, take a moment to jot down the number of clients this promotion brought in. At the end of the promotion, total all of the weekly results for a grand total of client responses to this promotion. Be sure to note bad weather, illness, or any mishaps that may have interfered with your promotion's potential success.)

Garden Club Manicures

Salon Name
Address
Phone

Invites all Garden Club members to
enjoy a relaxing manicure
at half-price all week!

Hurry Sale Ends __ /__ /__

Let us thank you for the beauty
you bring into our lives!

GARDEN CLUB MANICURE PROMOTION

Objective
✂ Reach new manicure and retail clients.

Description
✂ Offer a discount manicure to all garden club members. Send a copy of this promo, as a letter.

Preparation
✂ Meet with salon staff and explain the promo to everyone. Make copy of the tracking sheet.

Estimated Cost
✂ $20–30 if only flyers used.

PROMOTION TRACKING SHEET

(Keep This on a Clipboard at the Reception Desk)

_____
NAME OF PROMOTION

_____   _____
DATE PROMO STARTS   DATE PROMO ENDS

_____
AMOUNT OF NEW CUSTOMERS

	SUN	MON	TUE	WED	THU	FRI	SAT
Week 1							
Week 2							
Week 3							
Week 4							
Monthly Total							

(At the end of every day, take a moment to jot down the number of clients this promotion brought in. At the end of the promotion, total all of the weekly results for a grand total of client responses to this promotion. Be sure to note bad weather, illness, or any mishaps that may have interfered with your promotion's potential success.)

Realtors Deserve a Break

You spend long days on your feet,
so let us pamper you with
a pedicure and
foot and leg message!

Salon Name
Address
Phone

SAVE $4 THIS WEEK ONLY!

(Expiration Date)

After You Close The Sale,
Let Us Pamper Your Feet!

REALTORS PROMOTION

Objective
✄ Reach new pedicure clients.

Description
✄ Offer a discount pedicure to realtors. Send a letter to every realtor in town.

Preparation
✄ Create your own promotional flyer.

Meet with salon staff and explain the promo to everyone. Give all a stack of flyers to distribute.

Make copy of the tracking sheet.

Estimated Cost
✄ $20–30 if only flyers used. Additional cost for postage.

PROMOTION TRACKING SHEET

(Keep This on a Clipboard at the Reception Desk)

_____

NAME OF PROMOTION

_____   _____

DATE PROMO STARTS   DATE PROMO ENDS

_____

AMOUNT OF NEW CUSTOMERS

	SUN	MON	TUE	WED	THU	FRI	SAT
Week 1							
Week 2							
Week 3							
Week 4							
Monthly Total							

(At the end of every day, take a moment to jot down the number of clients this promotion brought in. At the end of the promotion, total all of the weekly results for a grand total of client responses to this promotion. Be sure to note bad weather, illness, or any mishaps that may have interfered with your promotion's potential success.)

Choir Members
Are Invited To A
"Members Only Sale"

Perms Half-Price

For choir members of:
(*choir name here*)

Salon Name
Address
Phone

Dates of Sale

Thanks for all the beautiful music your choir has given us!

CHOIR MEMBERS SPECIAL—PROMOTION

Objective
✂ Reach new clients.

Description
✂ Offer a discount to choir members.

Preparation
✂ Create your own promotional flyer and mail it to choir directors in the area.

Meet with salon staff and explain the promo to everyone. Give all a stack of flyers to distribute.

Make copy of the tracking sheet.

Estimated Cost
✂ $20–30 if only flyers used, additional cost for postage.

PROMOTION TRACKING SHEET

(Keep This on a Clipboard at the Reception Desk)

_____
NAME OF PROMOTION

_____   _____
DATE PROMO STARTS   DATE PROMO ENDS

_____
AMOUNT OF NEW CUSTOMERS

	SUN	MON	TUE	WED	THU	FRI	SAT
Week 1							
Week 2							
Week 3							
Week 4							
Monthly Total							

(At the end of every day, take a moment to jot down the number of clients this promotion brought in. At the end of the promotion, total all of the weekly results for a grand total of client responses to this promotion. Be sure to note bad weather, illness, or any mishaps that may have interfered with your promotion's potential success.)

Nothing But Smooth Sailing...

...When You Start Your Beach Trip,
With a Trip to Our Salon

Salon Name
Address
Phone

Sale In for *Savings of 25%*
On *all* haircuts for beach bound clients!

Bring us a copy of your beach reservations and
we will sail you into a whirlwind of a sale!

SMOOTH SAILING BEACH HAIRCUT PROMOTION

Objective
✂ Reach new clients. Help clients have easy haircare at the beach.

Description
✂ Offer a 25% on cuts when a reservation for a beach trip is presented.

Preparation
✂ **Two Months Before:** Create your own promotional flyer.

✂ **One Month Before:** Distribute flyers as bag stuffers (swimsuit stores, resorts, beach hotels, schools). Notify current clients by posting a flyer on your bulletin board for a month previous to the promotion.

Meet with salon staff and explain the promo to everyone. Give all a stack of flyers to distribute.

✂ **One Week Before:** Set up a retail display for sunscreen and conditioner.

✂ **One Day Before:** Review promo with staff. Make a copy of the tracking sheet.

Estimated Cost
✂ $20-30 if only flyers used. Additional cost for newspaper ad—depends on ad size and newspaper rates.

PROMOTION
TRACKING SHEET

(Keep This on a Clipboard at the Reception Desk)

NAME OF PROMOTION

DATE PROMO STARTS   DATE PROMO ENDS

AMOUNT OF NEW CUSTOMERS

	SUN	MON	TUE	WED	THU	FRI	SAT
Week 1							
Week 2							
Week 3							
Week 4							
Monthly Total							

(At the end of every day, take a moment to jot down the number of clients this promotion brought in. At the end of the promotion, total all of the weekly results for a grand total of client responses to this promotion. Be sure to note bad weather, illness, or any mishaps that may have interfered with your promotion's potential success.)

BON VOYAGE

Cruise into our salon
for a cool sale,
before you take a cruise!

Salon Name
Address
Phone

Sale in for savings of 25%
Just show us your ticket!

We will discount your perm 25%

CRUISE IN PROMOTION

Objective

✂ Reach new perm and retail clients. Help perms last longer at the beach or cruise! Reduce perm redos from abuse.

Description

✂ Offer a 25% discount when a cruise ship ticket presented.

Preparation

✂ **Two Months Before:** Place an ad in newspaper and get copy of the ad slick to use for flyers. (Buy neon paper to run flyers on.)

Check for co-op money with cruise lines.

✂ **One Month Before:** Distribute flyers as bag stuffers (swimsuit stores, resorts, beach hotels, travel agencies). Notify current clients by posting a flyer on your bulletin board for a month previous to the promotion.

Meet with salon staff and explain the promo to everyone. Give all a stack of flyers to distribute.

✂ **One Week Before:** Double check with the newspaper. Set up a retail display for sunscreen and conditioner.

✂ **One Day Before the Ad Runs:** Review promo with staff. Make copy of the tracking sheet.

Estimated Cost

✂ $20–30 if only flyers used. Additional cost for newspaper ad—depends on ad size and newspaper rates.

PROMOTION TRACKING SHEET

(Keep This on a Clipboard at the Reception Desk)

_____

NAME OF PROMOTION

_____   _____

DATE PROMO STARTS   DATE PROMO ENDS

_____

AMOUNT OF NEW CUSTOMERS

	SUN	MON	TUE	WED	THU	FRI	SAT
Week 1							
Week 2							
Week 3							
Week 4							
Monthly Total							

(At the end of every day, take a moment to jot down the number of clients this promotion brought in. At the end of the promotion, total all of the weekly results for a grand total of client responses to this promotion. Be sure to note bad weather, illness, or any mishaps that may have interfered with your promotion's potential success.)

glossary

Ad Slicks: The shiny copy of a printed ad, which can be used to make instant flyers.

Barter: Trading or exchanging your services with another, without exchanging money.

Brand Recognition: The name of a particular brand of product that has been promoted so successfully that the product's name is now synonymous with the product.

Break-Even Point: The amount of money that can be charged for a service that still allows a profit to be made.

Circulation: The number of customers served by a particular media—subscribers, listeners, or viewers reached.

Client Base: The group of clients you wish to attract, any group of people with a common need.

Client Concerns: Anything that makes your customer unhappy, uneasy, or anxious.

Collateral: Any printed, promotional materials that your client can hold in her hand.

Computer Graphics: Artwork that comes off a software program from a personal computer.

Co-op Advertising: Teaming up with a product manufacturer that helps you promote your services if you include its product in your promotion.

Customer Service: The manner in which you service customers, put-ting the customer's needs before anything else, every time the client enters your salon.

End Caps: Display and attention grabber at the end of an aisle.

Exposure: Using promotions to present yourself to the commu-nity as a stylist who is ready to accept and service new clients.

Image: Presentation or appear-ance you project to clients, a reflection of you and your tal-ents.

Loss Leader: An item sold at a ridiculously low price to lure customers to buy items you really want to sell.

Market: See *client base*. The group of people you wish to service in your salon.

Mission Statement: One or two ideas that sum up what you would like your salon to achieve and how you plan to reach that goal.

On-line Promotions: Putting coupons, sales information, and your address on a Web site on the Internet.

One Day Sale: Certificates for perms that are sold on only one day per year, yet are redeemable for an entire year.

Penetrate the Market: Using several media, at once, to cre-ate a campaign that helps clients associate your name with services.

Point of Sale (POS): Any printed materials that promote your business at the point where the customer makes a purchase.

Professional Courtesy: Receiv-ing or giving a free service from or to another stylist.

Referrals: Customers sent to you by someone else, often one of your clients or another stylist.

Retail Display: The display set up to promote retail items.

Salon Image: The way your salon portrays itself to clients, a composite of all the salon employees as well as the salon itself.

Sale-Only Clients: Clients who come to you only when you are offering a sale.

Selected Stylists: New or not-so-busy stylists who usually participate in sale offerings.

Software: Programs installed on a computer that allow specific functions with that computer; include spreadsheets, data bases, word processing pro-grams, and graphic design pro-grams.

Speed Bumps: Displays that slow customers down so that they have to go around your retail display to get in and out of the salon.

Tracking Sales: Keeping track of how many and what types of services and sales you do for a given time period—week, month, etc.

Transient Trade: Clients who walk into the salon or call for an appointment, for the first time, and do not request a spe-cific stylist.

Trend: The inclination or direc-tion things are moving toward.

Value Pricing: Same item or ser-vice offered in two salons and one provides it for a lower price; customers are consid-ered value-priced shoppers.

Velox: See *ad slick*. Older term meaning the same as ad slick.

Vision: The picture you place in your client's mind when you suggest a new concept, look or service.

index

A

Accountants, 24
Ad slicks, 54, 55, 64, 66
Adhesive tape, 65
Advertising agencies, 38, 39-40, 50
Anniversary celebrations, 32
Apartment complexes, 50, 65
Appearance, 21. See also
    Salon image
Appointment books, 26, 33
    See also Scheduling
Artists, 3
Awards, 39

B

Baby boomers, 18
Bad-weather promotions, 36
Balloons, 10, 17, 32
Bangs, 35
Banners, 41
Bargain hunters, 14-16, 20
Bartering, 56-57
Beauty product
    manufacturers, 54, 57
Beauty supply companies, 24
Beehive hairstyles, 18, 19
Billboards, 41, 42
Birthday cards, 32
Boutiques, 14, 56. See also
    Dress shops
Brand recognition, 25, 30,
    39-40, 43

Break-even point, 54, 56, 57,
    58, 59
Brochures, 29, 50. See also
    Flyers
Brushes, 49, 50
Budgets
    advertising agencies and,
        39
    defined, 24
    development of, 26-27,
        52-54
    sample, 25, 53
    television production and,
        43
    yearly calendars and, 46
Bulletin boards, 9, 50, 64, 65
Business cards, 3-4, 6, 33, 50
Business plans, 24-27, 46
Business professionals, 2, 9-10
Business trends, 26, 33

C

Calendars, 4, 29, 46-51, 52
Cameras, 3
Cellophane adhesive tape, 65
Cellular phones, 10
Certificates, 60-62. See also
    Gift certificates
Charities, 41, 56
Children, 14, 15, 16, 17-18
Christmas, 32, 42, 47
Churches, 14, 50
Circulation (media), 40, 45

City newspapers, 40, 50
Cleanliness, 22, 48
Client concerns, 34-35, 37
Clothesline displays, 48
Clothing, 22, 28, 35
Co-op advertising, 54, 55, 57
Coffee service, 60
Collateral advertising, 44, 45
College classes, 24, 64
College students, 43, 64
Color business cards, 4
Commercials, 42-43
Communication, 2, 35
Community bulletin boards,
    65
Community colleges, 24, 64
Complacency, 34
Complaints, 23, 34
Computer advertising, 43, 45
Computer graphics, 3, 64, 66
Computer hookups, 10
Conditioners, 18, 49
Conflict of interest, 39
Consultations, 5, 35
Contests, 28
Continuing education, 24
Cost estimation, 52-56.
    See also Budgets
Country club members, 9
Coupons, 43-44
    of drugstores, 49
    on flyers, 44, 63
    of large companies, 3

for new residents, 50
for pedicures, 56
for spouses, 10
in thank-you notes, 32
Courtesy, 23. *See also*
  Professional courtesies
Creative awards, 39
Credit card receipts, 60
Customer Appreciation
  Days, 32
Customer service, 22–23,
  27, 30
Customers
  complaints of, 23, 34
  professional, 2, 9–10
  records for, 33, 35
  referrals of, 5–6, 7, 32, 33
  retail displays and, 48–49
  retention of, 31–37
  sale-only, 59, 62
  salon appearance and, 22
  walk-in, 1, 7, 14

D

Day spas, 10
Demographics, 40, 42.
  See also Market
Department stores, 49
Discount stores, 14
Discount trees, 32
Discounts
  on bad-weather days, 36
  break-even point for, 54,
    56, 57, 58, 59
  card offers of, 4
  for current clients, 32, 33
  handwritten tags for, 49
  for older adults, 18
  for referrals, 6, 32
  in specialty salons, 16–17
  for upscale clients, 9–10
Doctors, 9
Dress shops, 29. *See also*
  Boutiques
Dressing rooms, 22
Drugstore shampoo coupons,
  49

Duo-product displays, 49

E

Early-morning appointments,
  9, 18
Employee relocation, 50
End caps, 48, 51
Estheticians, 5, 6
Exposure, 2–3, 7
Eye makeup, 48

F

Facial tissue, 3, 26
Facial treatments, 10, 16, 17
Family achievements, 32
Family specials, 11, 12, 16–17,
  50
Fashion shows, 14, 56
Fashion trends, 18, 20
Fax machines, 10
Fears, 34
Fingernail technicians, 5, 6
Fitness centers, 14, 65
Floor advertising, 44, 49
Floor sweeping, 22
Flowers, 10, 32
Flyers, 3, 63–66
  coloring of, 14, 15
  coupons on, 44, 63
  for family specials, 12
  in market penetration, 39
  for middle-income
    prospects, 11
  for one-day sales, 60
  for open-house
    promotions, 50
  for value-priced salons, 16
Fold-open cards, 4
Food, 17. *See also* Coffee
  service
Free merchandise, 3, 18, 32, 49
Free services, 6
  consultations, 5, 35
  haircuts, 32, 33, 43, 49–50
  manicures, 56
  shampoo styles, 57
Frozen fruit-juice treats, 3

G

Gift certificates, 9–10, 18, 48, 60
Graphics software, 3, 64, 66
Gray hair, 18
Greenhouses, 32

H

Hair clippings, 22
Hair color services
  best-selling, 59
  consultation on, 5
  potential provision of, 23
  retail promotion and, 48
  seasonal promotion of, 47
  staff contests for, 28
  suggestion of, 35
Hair conditioners, 18, 49
Hair ornaments, 48
Hair services, 24
Hairbrushes, 49, 50
Haircuts
  by specialty salons, 16–17
  for middle-income
    clientele, 11
  free, 32, 33, 43, 49–50
  radio advertising of, 42
  seasonal promotion of, 47
  supplements to, 23
  tracking of, 34
  See also Shampoo styles
Hairpieces, 49
Hairspray, 51
Half-price discounts.
  See Discounts
Handouts. *See* Brochures;
  Flyers
Handwritten tags, 49
Hanukkah, 32
Health clubs, 14, 65
High school students, 64
Holidays, 42, 65. *See also*
  Christmas
Home pages (Internet), 43
Human resources
  departments, 50, 65

I

Ice cream coupons, 18
Illustrations. *See* Pictures
Image. *See* Personal
appearance; Salon image
Industry newspapers, 40
Instant cameras, 3
Internet, 43, 45

J

Jeans, 5
Jewelers, 56

K

Key chains, 32, 50

L

Labor costs, 54, 56
Laptop computers, 10
Laundromats, 65
Libraries, 24
Local events, 29, 47–48, 64–65
Local newspapers, 40, 50
Local organizations, 14, 20, 29, 50
Local stores, 14, 29, 49, 56. *See also* Supermarkets
Logos, 5, 63
Long-distance calls, 50
Loss leaders, 48–49, 51
Lunchtime specials, 9

M

Magazine advertisements, 40–41
Magnetic signs, 42. *See also* Refrigerator magnets
Mail offers, 43
Mailboxes, 65
Mailing lists, 11
Makeovers, 2, 11
Malls, 65
Managers, 2, 5
Manicures, 24, 56
Manufacturers, 54, 57
Market, 8–20. *See also* Customers; Demographics
Market penetration, 39, 45
Massage, 10
Media, 11, 38–45
Medical professionals, 9, 64
Men's salons, 17
Middle-income salons, 10–14
Mission statements, 27, 30
Monthly promotions, 46–47, 52, 53
Mother's Day, 10, 32, 64
Mousse, 55
Music, 23, 42

N

Nail files, 32
Nail technicians, 5, 6
National magazines, 40–41
Neighborhood stores. *See* Local stores
New citizens clubs, 50
New-in-town promotions, 49–50
Newsletters, 50
Newspaper advertisements, 40
co-op, 54, 55, 57
for one-day sales, 60
for photo shoots, 11
for value-priced salons, 16
Newspaper articles, 32
Newspaper columns, 50
Nurses, 9, 64

O

Older clients, 18–20
On-line advertising, 43, 45
One-day sales, 60–62
Open-house promotions, 50
Outdoor advertising, 41–42
Overbookings, 5, 6
Overhead, 54, 56

P

Paint damage, 65
Pamphlets. *See* Brochures
Patrons. *See* Customers
Pedicures, 56
Permanent waves
best-selling, 59
discounts for, 54, 56
for gray hair, 18
market penetration for, 39
one-day sales of, 60, 61
potential provision of, 23
retail promotion and, 48
seasonal promotion of, 47
spiral, 20
suggestion of, 35
television advertising of, 43
tracking of, 34
Personal appearance, 21
Photography, 11, 18, 19, 28, 44
Pictures, 63. *See also* Computer graphics; Videos
Point of sale, 44, 45
Politeness. *See* Courtesy
Polyurethane, 44
Posters, 44, 48
Preparation sheets, 52–53, 56, 59
Press releases, 41, 50
Product manufacturers, 54, 57
Product recognition, 25, 30, 39–40, 43
Product suppliers, 24
Professional beauticians
appearance of, 21
consultation with, 46–47
retail products and, 34
teamwork with, 5–6, 22
training of, 24, 27–29, 34
Professional clientele, 2, 9–10
Professional courtesies, 2, 7
PTAs, 14, 56

R

Radio advertisements, 42
Reception areas, 22
Referrals, 5–6, 7, 32, 33
Refrigerator calendars, 29
Refrigerator magnets, 4. *See also* Magnetic signs

Refunds, 23
Retail displays, 22, 48–49, 51
Retail products
  in children's salons, 18
  flyers with, 14
  promotions of, 48–49
  sale-only clients and, 59
  tracking of, 33, 34

S

Sale-only clientele, 59, 62
Sales, 11, 31, 42, 58–62. *See also* Discounts
Sales checks, 60
Salon image, 2, 7, 21, 22, 23
SalonOvations' Guide to Salon Promotions and Client Retention (Hoffman), 23
Sample merchandise, 3, 18, 32, 49
Sandals, 56
Savings accounts, 60
Scheduling, 10. *See also* Appointment books; Early-morning appointments; Overbookings
School newspapers, 40
Schools, 11, 64, 65. *See also* Community colleges; PTAs
SCORE (Service Corps of Retired Executives), 24
Seasonal promotions, 47–48. *See also* Holidays
Selected stylists, 59–60, 62
Senior clients, 18–20
Shampoo areas, 22, 44, 48
Shampoo styles, 57
Shampoos, 18, 48–49, 50
Shoe stores, 14, 56
Shopping centers, 65
Signs, 41–42
Skin care, 10, 16, 17
Small-town newspapers, 40, 50

Software (computers), 3, 64, 66
Soliciting, 65
Special discounts. *See* Discounts; Sales
Special events. *See* Local events
Specialty salons, 16–20
Specialty stores. *See* Boutique
Speed bumps (retail displays), 49, 51
Spiral perms, 20
Sports menus, 11, 13–14, 17
Sports newspapers, 40
Sports seasons, 47–48
Staff. *See* Professional beauticians
State fair concepts, 48
Stores. *See* Local stores
Students, 43, 64
Suntan products, 48
Supermarkets, 44, 48, 49, 65
Suppliers, 24
Sweeping, 22

T

Take-out food, 17
Teamwork, 5–6, 22. *See also* Co-op advertising
Teenage salons, 18
Telephone cards, 50
Telephone greetings, 23
Television advertisements, 42–43
Tennis flyers, 65
Testimonials, 43
Thank-you notes, 32
Time considerations, 34. *See also* Scheduling
Tissue, 3, 26
Toys, 17, 18
Tracking sales, 33–34, 37
Trade newspapers, 40
Trade shows, 24

Training, 24, 27–29, 34
Transient trade, 1, 7, 14
Trends, 18, 20, 26, 33
Trespassing, 65

U

Upscale clientele, 2, 9–10

V

Value pricing, 14–16, 20
Velox (ad slicks), 54, 55, 64, 66
Videos, 28–29
Vision, 35, 37

W

Waiting rooms, 22
Walk-in clientele, 1, 7, 14
Water toys, 18
"We miss you" notes, 33
Web sites (Internet), 43, 45
Wedding rings, 56
Weekly newspapers, 40
Welcome Wagons, 49
Wig cleaner, 49
Window dressing, 49
Windshields, 65
Worksheets, 52–53, 56, 59
Workstations, 22. *See also* Shampoo areas

Y

Yearly budgets, 52–54
Yearly calendars, 46–51, 52